Angels at War

by William Kitchen

Contents

Introduction

This piece is included in my story to let you know who we were and what we did. It is copied from the pages of the "Voice of the Angels," and that in turn is copied from the book "The Angels" by General Flanagan – an excellent summary of the 11ᵗʰ Airborne in the Pacific War.

The 11ᵗʰ Airborne division was an unusual unit in an unconventional theater in an unconventional atmosphere and commanded by an unconventional commanding general. It was the only airborne division in the Pacific Theater, and because it was "Airborne" it had only just over half of the men and fire power of the conventional infantry divisions fighting in that theater. With Napoleonic mimicry, it equalized its small size and light equipment by its self-imposed, imagined and real, superior fighting quality. Nonetheless, because it was a division, commanded by a major general just as were the standard infantry and mechanized divisions, the senior commanders under whom it fought (MacArthur, Eichelberger, and Griswald) thought of it as a division, and gave it full size division missions. Thus, the 11ᵗʰ, in all its months of fighting on Leyte and Luzon, never enjoyed the extravagance afforded to the other divisions in combat units in reserve. The conventional triangular fighting concept of "two up and one back" was a luxury the 11ᵗʰ simply could not afford. The division was indeed unconventional.

The unconventional atmosphere of the war in the Pacific derived from the enemy's tactics, from his fanaticism and his willingness to self destruct for his emperor, his country, and his religion. Our men considered it their duty and privilege to assist the Japanese soldier in this effort. In Europe for example, there were generally front lines behind which most support units were relatively safe from attack (except in such cases as the German 1944 Battle of the Bulge offensive). For the most part the front lines in Europe were relatively linear and fairly solid. As the Allies moved forward, they overran enemy positions and killed, captured, or drove back the defenders. In the Pacific Theater, however, there were no such conventional front lines. The area between the U.S. Infantry and the supporting artillery was a no man's land, and the *artillery and troops farther to the so called rear had to protect themselves – especially at night – with their own 360° perimeter. They were well dug in and were defended with scrounged up machine guns and even, as in the case of the 457th FA[1] Battalion, captured Japanese "knee" mortars. When an infantry unit stopped attacking for the night, it had to dig in, bring in protective mortar and artillery fires around itself, and prepare for the often suicidal attacks of the small groups of enemy foot troops, laden with bombs and grenades. This was especially true on Luzon when the enemy began to realize that he was not winning the war.*

The division was commanded by an unconventional, shrewd tactician who felt that because the troops were so good and so well trained, they could and would do all that was asked of them – and more. Who else but General Swing would have tried and succeeded in moving an artillery battalion to an area totally inaccessible by road by borrowing a C-47 air/sea rescue ship and parachuting his howitzers and men into the area? Who else would have had the foresight and temerity to use his augmented fleet of sixteen cub aircraft to establish an airborne logistical tramway to back up his troops who were fighting without a land-based logistical tail?

At peak operation, the sixteen cubs carried twenty one tons a day to their airhead at Manarawat on Leyte. Who else would divorce an artillery battalion and engineers and other assorted non-infantry types from their guns, miniature bulldozers, D-handled shovels, and typewriters and use them to attack an elite Japanese parachute battalion that had had the effrontery to drop on the headquarters of the 11th Airborne Division at Burauen, Leyte?

Who had the confidence in his men to know, without a doubt, such an attack would succeed? Who else would accept as perfectly normal and without discussion or question the mission of invading southern Luzon by amphibious and parachute attack as the sum total of the eighth army? And who else would accept as perfectly routine and unremarkable the task of freeing and evacuating over 2000 civilian prisoners held in a secure environment some forty-five miles deep in enemy held territory and guarded by perhaps as

---

[1] Field Artillery

many as 250 Japanese security forces, knowing there were between 8,000 and 15,000 more Japanese forces within a couple of hours march to the camp? Major General Joseph M. Swing, the unconventional commander of the 11th, that's who.

A little note from a recent edition of The Voice:

Avengers of Bataan

Although our good friends in the 38th Infantry Division bear this nickname, they merely retook the ground of Bataan during the Luzon campaign. But the 11th Airborne engaged and destroyed the two imperial Japanese divisions (the 16th and 26th) who were responsible for the atrocities of the Bataan Death March. The 11th Airborne wiped them out in the miserable mountains of Leyte.

How in the world did a military outfit get to be called "**The Angels**?" It happened this way:

A nun, concerned about and wanting to get away from the miseries of life in a Japanese prison was praying about her situation. At the end of her prayer time she said, "If *God* is going to get us out of this, He will have to send the angels." Later, when she saw the healthy, well fed, well dressed young men coming down out of the sky on parachutes, she was awestruck, and said, "He sent the angels!" We heard about it and we grabbed it. And we – the 11th Airborne – have claimed to be *The Angels* ever after.

Angels at War

(From the address that Henry DeVries gave at the 1999 reunion banquet in Portland, Oregon.)

It is true that war brings out the worst in some people. It is also true that war brings out the best in some people. The first example of the latter is best found in the story of the DeVries family.

Henry told us that he went into the prison as a 120 pound twelve year old and came out as a 78 pound fifteen year old.

The senior DeVries went to the Philippines as missionaries during the nineteen-twenties. All their children were born in the Philippines and educated in Philippine schools.

When the family went into prison there was inadequate food and poor sanitation. Sixteen year old Jean got dysentery and there was no medicine available. She was only getting worse. She was reduced to trying the native remedy of chewing charcoal from the fire pit, swallowing it and hoping that as it went through the system it would scour out the disease and thus remove it. It was not working.

About this time Henry, because he was a child, was allowed to go outside the prison and gather wood scraps for a cooking fire. As he was gathering wood he recognized his Philippine teacher being escorted by three armed Japanese soldiers. The teacher was carrying something that the Japanese wanted moved, and had compelled this teacher to move for them. As the teacher passed by Henry he managed to drop his burden and while gathering it up he asked Henry "How is the family?" Henry replied "All the family is well except Jean. Jean is very bad with dysentery." Of course the teacher had to go on and finish his job for the Japanese.

That night Mr. DeVries senior felt the teacher's hand on his shoulder and a six ounce coke bottle of warm, fresh, sweet goat's milk was placed in his hand. He was told, "It's for Jean." This happened for three nights and Jean got well. Teachers know and care for their students.

How do you evaluate this gift? There was a curfew and anyone found outside after curfew would have been shot. This man not only was out too late, he observed the prison so that he knew where to find the family. He then avoided the guards and entered the prison. He not only gave Jean what she needed but he took that milk from his own family who also needed food. The goat was kept inside the chicken house out of sight after wandering Japanese soldiers had shot their cow for no reason. They wanted to preserve the goat so they cut grass by hand and fed her out of sight.

An Angel? I think so.

~~~

From the book *That We Might Live* by Grace Nash[2]

Next is the story of Grace Nash and Hough Williams.

Grace was a concert violinist. She was married to a mining engineer. He was employed at a mine in northern Luzon Island. So they lived in the Philippines. They had a family – two boys ages five and seven. A third boy was born in the prison.

Again the food was inadequate and baby food was totally nonexistent. So the only food for their baby was breast milk, and of course the starving mother could not provide a good supply of breast milk. The boy was alive but not thriving. One fact of life in the prison was the standing in line, which they had to do in order to get any water. The father could not do this because the Japanese had him on a job where he had to work, and you can't leave an infant with a pair of five and seven year old boys. So she took all her boys with her to stand in line for water.

There she met Hough Williams, a British sailor who had been to sea for many years, and he looked the part. He told the boys fantastic stories about cannibals, pirates, ship wrecks and whatever else he dreamed up. The boys loved it.

Then one day Hough did not show up. He was gone several days and Grace wondered what had become of him. Then one day as she was in line Hough came up to her and placed in her hand a two gallon container of powdered milk. She said to him "Oh

---

[2] Shano Publishing, January, 1985

Hough! You need that – for she knew he was starving, too. His reply, "Nah, never touch the stuff. It's for the wee one."

"But oh, Hough I have nothing. I can never repay you in any way."

"Oh yes you can. Play me Danny Boy at your next concert." (Think of the precious value of music.)

Grace had given concerts for the prisoners, but due to the stress in her life she did not intend to give any more. Now she was obligated to do one more concert. She prepared and even placed a chair of honor in the front row for Hough. Hough did not show up. So as soon as she could, she went to the men's section to inquire about him. She learned that he had died that afternoon. She also learned that during his absence from the water line he had been wrestling with a decision – give the milk or keep the milk. Finally he decided on the self sacrificing action of giving the milk. She also learned that to try to supplement his diet he had been eating roots from plants in the ground hoping to gain a little nourishment from them. It was considered that those roots were likely the cause of his death.

An angel? I think so. Do your eyes have tears in them? Mine do.

~~~

From the book Escape at Dawn, by Carol Terry, is the story of Mrs. Sileen. She was in prison with her three daughters. No mention is made of any husband.

During the initial fight for control of the Los Banos prison, Mrs. Sileen's twelve year old daughter received a bullet wound in the abdomen (in one side and out the other). She was bleeding and could not walk due to beriberi– a starvation condition – and for the same reason the mother could not carry her.

The paratroopers had set the buildings on fire because they wanted the prisoners to move quickly. There was a ten thousand man Japanese force only eight miles away and they were thirty five miles from the front line in Japanese territory. A trooper was assigned to go through each building and see to it that nobody was left behind in a burning building. Mrs. Sileen asked that trooper for help. He told her to take the other two girls and go to the transportation.

"We will take care of this one," he said.

She said, "I cannot leave my bleeding and wounded daughter in a burning building."

He told her that if she did not take the other two girls and go that she and the girls would all die in the burning building. Again he said, "We will take care of this one."

Can you imagine the stress and burden that was on the mind of that mother? She did take the other girls and go. Later the wounded twelve year old was found among the evacuated prisoners. The soldier had kept his word.

Beriberi

Beriberi is caused by a deficit in thiamine (Vitamin B1). Common symptoms include weight loss, emotional disorders, weakness, limb pain, irregular heart rate, and swelling of bodily tissues. It may, in extreme cases, cause cardiac failure and death. There are three basic types:
• Dry beriberi is characterized by severe weight loss and partial paralysis.
• Wet beriberi affects the heart and nervous system
• Infantile beriberi is characterized by moaning, hoarseness, vomiting, diarrhea, and convulsions; death is common.
Historically, Beriberi has been widespread in regions dependent on what is variously referred to as polished, white, or de-husked rice. This type of rice has its husk removed in order to extend its lifespan, but also has the unintended side-effect of removing the primary source of thiamine.

From Wikipedia, the Free Encyclopedia

An angel? Or just doing his duty?

You decide and whichever you decide, this is just one of the reasons that I am proud of my outfit – the 11th Airborne Division.

~~~

From personal conversation with Mr. John Blaylock:
John was a thirty-seven year old man. He had been a missionary in China. His mission had called him back to the U.S. due to approaching war clouds. Before he left China, a Chinese woman begged him to take with him her three children – children of her and her American husband, a military man who had been

stationed in China and was now not living. She knew that even though these children had an American father they would not have American citizenship unless they lived in America before they were eighteen years old. She, a Chinese woman would have a hard time even providing for them, and she could certainly never get them to the U.S. Thus John Blaylock had three children with him when he was trapped in Manila by the war.

In a video of Sally, who was an eleven year old at liberation time, she says, "At an early age I could catch, clean and eat a rat."

John, a healthy man, was assigned to a job cutting wood for the camp. This consisted of work away from the prison, accompanied by Japanese guards. One day at work, the Japanese guards purchased a coconut from a vendor. They gave the coconut to John, and even loaned him their bayonet to use in opening the nut. They warned him that if a Japanese officer should approach that he must immediately drop the nut and go to work. Because, if they were caught helping a prisoner they would receive very severe punishment. He agreed. They did not get caught. John ate the coconut.

Angels? With Japanese faces? **Yes.**

~ Please see Los Banos Prison Camp sketch on the next page ~

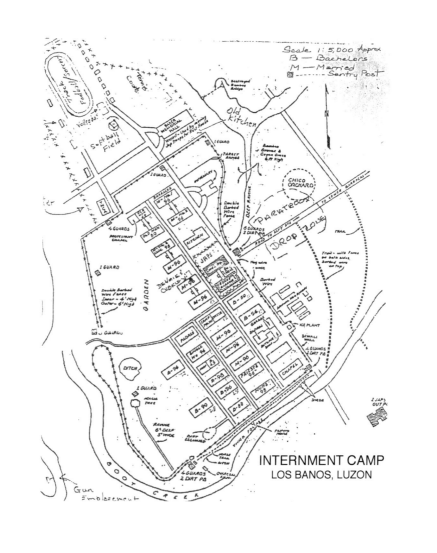

INTERNMENT CAMP
LOS BANOS, LUZON

Training
1943 Knollwood Maneuvers
by William Kitchen

The Voice of the Angels just recently printed a story from General Johnson about the *Knollwood Maneuvers* and their importance to the airborne concept in WWII for the United States.

Both Russia and Germany had used airborne troops in the past, and Germany used paratroopers to invade Crete. The last operation was successful, but expensive; about 20% casualties. Hitler never again used a large scale airborne operation.

Then came our invasion of Sicily, which again was successful, but costly. I read in one report that there were 66% casualties. Be that true or not, I have in front of me a copy of *The Glider Gang* by Milton Dank, a WWII glider pilot. In his book he tells of one flight of 144 gliders leaving Africa, of which only 54 reached Sicily, and of those 54 only 12 reached their assigned drop zones, but, *they took and held their objective.*

Early in WWII the U.S. was ready to radically change their airborne policies, severely limiting the use of gliders. General Swing and others worked to prevent those changes. Then came the Knollwood story, and I hereby submit my personal memories of that event.

My memories are in three parts, first the maneuver as it was seen by my wife.

I had been stationed in North Carolina. Due to a shortage of funds, Marge and I had looked around for inexpensive housing, and were so fortunate as to meet the Batchelor family, who took in my wife as a border, charging us $5 per week for her room and board. Later, just before the *Knollwood Maneuvers*, she had moved 100 yards down the road to the home of the Collins family. Somehow I had learned that the Batchelor farm was to be our drop zone, and I told her so.

When the gliders began landing in the corn field she went outside, not telling the Collins family, and she stood in the road and watched and heard the gliders come in. She tells of hearing the whistle of the wind in the struts, and then of hearing the crash and splintering of wood. She knew that I was in one of those gliders and had to have been worried. Once the gliders were on the ground, though, she could not see anything of them.

Later she stood outside and watched the tow planes come in and pick up the gliders that were able to be picked up.

Thus, my wife Marge has some very real memories of what came to be known as the *Knollwood Maneuvers.*

> **Glider Retrieval ~ "The Snatch"**
>
> Richard C. duPont, a 1930s glider soaring champion, demonstrated to U.S. Air Crops in 1941 that retrieval of gliders on the ground was feasible from the air. In the system the tow plane approached a pick-up station from a 45° angle, about twenty feet above the ground, with an airspeed of 130 to 145 mph depending on the weight of the glider. When the glider's tow rope was snagged by the plane's trailing hook, a winch drum in the tow plane began rapidly to feed out cable, then more slowly as a brake took effect. The weight of the glider slowed the tow plane to about 105 mph. Some of the initial shock to both planes was absorbed by the winch cable and the elasticity of the nylon tow rope.
>
> In about seven seconds the glider would accelerate from 0 to the speed of the tow plane and become airborne in as little as sixty feet. The cable drum braked to a full stop and then reversed. The glider, now 500 or more feet behind the tow plane, was slowly winched in to the tow rope hook.
>
> *Compiled by Leon B. Spencer, former WWII Glider Pilot*

~~~

The second part of my memories has to do with Captain Dick Hoyt. Captain Hoyt may correct me to say that the occasion was another night maneuver and not the big *Knollwood Maneuver.*

We had ridden out to the airport in a truck that contained a glider load, and all of our truckload got into one glider. We were alphabetically loaded into the gliders. There was Hoyt, the company commander riding in the copilot's seat. The others were George Imrich, Johnson, Heltso, Kitchen, and others.

We were seated in the glider waiting to take off, the tow ropes hooked up, the planes running up their motors, and I was foolishly engaging in "gallows humor" and asking Heltso what kind of flowers he wanted for his funeral. He was returning the same sort of talk to me.

I was on the left side of the glider front seat, and Heltso was seated on the right side of the glider, front seat facing me. Just as we were about to take off, a couple of radiomen came running up with a machine gun cart loaded with radio gear. They tied it down to the D-rings in the floor just in front of my seat. I knew that I could not put my feet on those radio tubes and I was trying to find a suitable place for them when Captain Atwood stuck his head inside the glider and told me, "You get in that glider over there."

There was no room for discussion. I got in the other glider. I was not very happy with the change because in that glider was a jeep, loaded with radio equipment. There was a driver, maybe Jessie P. Mickelson, and an officer, possibly Lieutenant Mabbatt.

The center rear seat was filled with a radio set, the right fender was filled with a power pack, and the left fender behind the driver was empty , so I sat there. I had a piece of the aircraft jabbing me in the right shoulder, but I made the flight in this manner. We landed okay. I then learned that the glider I had gotten out of had crashed.

Heltso and another man were killed.

Heltso was my friend, and I felt pretty crummy about the gallows humor I had engaged in. I decided then that I never want to joke about death like that again. A simple, short hour after my foolish talk, and my friend Heltso was dead.

Sometimes the thing that is good for you is not convenient for you.

Captain Hoyt, also on the crashed glider, was injured and had to leave the company.

~~~

My third memory from the *Knollwood Maneuvers* was as we came in for our landing.

As we landed, I heard something hitting the belly of the glider. I was scared, for I had walked over the drop zone, and I knew it was the Batchelor farm. They had a corn field, a tobacco field, a cotton field, and a watermelon patch. Just across the creek was a pine forest, and over in the corner of the farm were two stone silos. I certainly did not want to have any contact with them.

I thought the things hitting the glider were pine trees, because I did not think that corn could possibly make so much noise. But, we were okay, and *had* landed in the corn field, and right beside us was another glider with a radio in it.

The radio was likely an SCR-299, which was normally mounted on a six by six truck. The truck usually towed a trailer, and on the trailer was a generator for the radio powered by an engine about the size of a Jeep motor.

SCR–299 Radio

The SCR-299 "mobile communications unit" was developed to provide long-range communications during World War II. It was first used on November 8, 1942 during Operation TORCH to establish a radio net between beach landed forces and bases in Gibraltar. The range of the SCR-299 often exceeded the original specifications, sometime establishing contact over 2,300 miles.

War correspondents and press reporters frequently made use of the SCR-299 and later the SCR-399. Access to the sets was provided to them by units of the U.S. Army Group Communications Teams, and in one instance, the SCR-399 became the only means of getting press copy directly to London. The SCR-299 was heavy and large, requiring either a van or truck to carry it.

From Wikipedia, the Free Encyclopedia

Of course the truck and trailer setup was too big and bulky for a glider, so only the radio was mounted in it.[3]

Two big signalmen, I think they were Orville Matheny and Richard LaChance, climbed up on the wings of the radio glider. They took axes and started to chop off the wings. The glider pilot came unglued, and I heard him yell, "I put this overloaded glider in here without a scratch and now you are not going to chop off its wings!"

Captain Atwood turned, pointed behind us, and said, "Henry Stimson don't seem to be worried about it."

I looked that way and saw a staff car, next to which were three men in overcoats, standing there watching us. I assumed that one of them was indeed Henry Stimson, Secretary of War under President Franklin D. Roosevelt.

Gentlemen, we were under high class observation.

As soon as the wings were chopped off, the men picked up the tail of that glider and set it into the back of a jeep. Now the signal company had their big radio, and it was mobile. That jeep pulled that glider around on its own wheels for several days. I think that was an example of airborne thinking, figuring out a way to complete a task, and then doing it. I'm sorry that I do not, and never did have, a picture of that thing.

Back to my own personal part: We got the message center set up and were sending and receiving messages. We got word that one of our units had been overrun by the enemy, and that all of our code books had been compromised, so I spent the entire night under a bunch of shelter halves buttoned together making up new code books. This was all done in long hand in small notebooks provided for the purpose. I remember that I sat on the ground and

---

[3] In the booklet entitled *11ᵗʰ Airborne Division,* which came out before we went overseas, there is a picture in the section on the signal company. It shows that radio, mounted in the glider, with Ray Ellis all bundled up and operating it.

used my knees for a desk. I had to make a new book for every message center unit in the division. I finished just as the sun was coming up the next morning. I wonder now what did I have for light?

Other than these incidents, I have few memories of *Knollwood*. I just know that I wandered around in the woods for a few days and tried to stay dry as best I could. Afterwards, I was very glad to get on the trucks to go back to those tarpaper shacks with coal stoves in them. They looked and felt pretty good to me.

Training
Gliders and Where they Came From

(From a letter by William Kitchen in the mid-1980s)

I am doing this from memory, so it will not be a word for word match with my speech, but it will be close. The subject was gliders; my source material was mostly *The Glider Gang* by Milton Dank, a glider pilot.

I was mostly interested in the military glider, which seems to be the brainchild of the German flier Kurt Student, who was a pilot of both bombers and fighters for Germany during World War I.

After the war, according to the Versailles Treaty[4], Germany was not supposed to have much of an air force. However, Student did train a number of people to fly gliders, which gave him no problem with the League of Nations. However, it did create a pool of fliers who could be trained as power pilots, which is just what Hitler did when he decided to ignore the rest of the world and build up his military.

During this time Student watched the Russians put a whole division of men into a field at one time from tri-motored planes – paratroopers. He realized the value of that procedure, and at the same time realized that they were short on firepower. He thought that his gliders could support the paratroopers with heavier weapons, but he could not sell the idea to Hitler.

Now occurs one of those apparently insignificant events that eventually changes history. A German lady flier named Hanna Reitch once said to Hitler, "They are utterly silent in flight," and Hitler tucked that away in the back of his mind.

---

[4] Signed on June 28, 1919, though the actual fighting had ended on November 11, 1918. The treaty forbade Germany from pilot training in the conventional sense, but allowed glider training.

Later when he wanted to invade France, he had to go through by way of Belgium's Fort of Eben Emael, which had been built expressly to prevent Germany from going through. That stumped him. Though it was a tough obstacle to pass, Hitler did not want to send his tanks against the 120mm cannon, he did not want to send his paratroopers against the anti-aircraft guns, and he did not want to be held up by a long fight.

Then he remembered the words of Hanna Reitch. He called in Kurt Student, and sent him with ten gliders of soldiers using the German *DFS-230* gliders.[5] They were so narrow that they had only one bench seat, which the passengers straddled and sat in tandem with each other. That group was able to land without opposition on the roof of Eban Emael, where the guns of the fort could not lower enough to hit them. They blasted all of the pill boxes, held the infantry inside the fort, and in twenty four hours the fort surrendered. The world did not know what gliders were, and most thought that Hitler had employed saboteurs to take the fort.

> **Fort of Eben-Emael**
>
> The Battle of Fort Eben-Emael was a battle between Belgian and German forces that took place between 10 and 11 May 1940. Belgium's Eben-Emael fortress artillery pieces dominated several important bridges over the Albert Canal. German forces intended to use those bridges to advance into Belgium. The battle was a decisive victory for the German forces, with their airborne troops landing on top of the fortress via the use of gliders. The German troops then used explosives and flame-throwers to disable the outer defenses of the fortress. German forces were then able to utilize two bridges over the Albert Canal to bypass a number of Belgian defensive positions, and thus advance into Belgium in their invasion of the country. Once Belgium was successfully invaded, Germany had access to the port of Antwerp and was able to advance into Northern France.
>
> *From Wikipedia, the Free Encyclopedia*

---

[5] The DFS 230 was developed in 1933; it could carry nine soldiers and their equipment, a payload of about 2600 pounds.

Then Student prepared a glider force to use in the invasion of England, which never happened, so, wanting to employ his brainchild he convinced Hitler to use them on the invasion of Crete. He did take that island mostly by the use of airborne troops paratroopers and gliders. But it was a very expensive operation. Of 25,000 men committed to the conflict the casualty list was 5,000. Hitler said, "It is too expensive," and he never again used large airborne units.

By now England and America were looking at gliders; the first British glider looked a lot like the German glider. They built others, the *Airspeed Horsa*[6] glider, for instance, with an 88 foot wing span carried 30 soldiers. To unload a big item like a jeep or artillery piece required the unbolting of the tail section. People did not like to do that under fire, and some took axes or saws along to speed up the job. One crew took primer cord[7], and they got the tail off from that glider in very short time, but their cargo was set on fire and destroyed. That was a real labor saving idea; they did not even have to pick up the pieces to unload them. So, it seems that the words glider and trouble sort of go together.[8]

Then the British built the Hamilcar glider[9] with a wingspan of 110 feet and a load capacity of 18 tons. They hauled small tanks in them, but due to a design flaw it was necessary to let the air out of the tires and drain the oil out of the struts to unload the thing.

---

[6] Airspeed AS.51 Horsa was named after *Horsa*, the fifth century conqueror of Great Britain.

[7] Primer cord, also known as Detonation Cord (Det cord), is an explosive material used to detonate high explosives.

[8] I saw the Horsa glider at McCall but thank God I did not have to ride it.

[9] The General Aircraft Limited (GAL) 49 Hamilcar was made mostly of wood, primarily birch and spruce.

That made the Waco CG-4A[10] American glider look pretty good, with its hinge at the top of the nose so that the nose could swing up and let the cargo out pretty fast.

The American production line was full, and none of the big outfits wanted to build gliders, they were busy with other things like bombers, tanks, and so forth. The gliders were built by furniture makers and piano makers, one casket maker, or anybody who thought they might build one. In St. Louis, Missouri, the mayor, part of the city council, and some military people went for a demonstration ride in the "new industry of the city." At about three thousand feet a wing fell off, and all aboard were killed. The casket maker had figured out a cheaper way to attach the wing.

Believe it or not, a number of men wanted to fly the things; volunteers came from many places. One army man wanted to volunteer, but his commanding officer would not approve the application, saying his job as a draftsman was too important to let him go, so he spilled ink on one blue print, rubbed holes in another and "lost" another, after which his application was approved. At least that one man was determined.

America got into the glider wars with the invasion of Sicily, where everything went wrong. There were high winds, and the 300 foot long nylon ropes which had been used in Africa and laid out in the sun began to break as soon as they started to go out over the ocean. Some planes used poor navigation and lost their way. Others flew over the American fleet and were shot down by our own people.

Other things went wrong. For instance, one flight of 144 gliders left Africa to go to Sicily, but only 54 of them reached Sicily. I think only four reached their assigned drop zones. One of the drop zones was the bridge at Ponte Grande; they took that bridge and held it over night with 30 men, lost it

---

[10] The Waco CG-4A glider was made of wood and metal covered with fabric. 13,900 CG-4As were produced by sixteen companies between 1942 and 1945.

briefly the next day to tanks, and with other help retook and held it the next day.

Due to the high casualty rate at Sicily the American brass was ready to dump the Airborne concept, at least as to division strength, but maybe keep as much as Battalion strength units. General Swing and others wanted to keep the division size units. A demonstration of division capabilities was set up, which was the Knollwood maneuvers; we knew nothing of those decisions at high places.

In war or even in maneuvers one person can see only a small portion of what is going on, a few yards left, a few right, and a few ahead, and that is it. I certainly could not see the big picture. However the powers that be declared that the Knollwood maneuvers were a success. Without a doubt the Airforce did drop most of us at the right place at the right time, and we did receive supplies for a few days.

My own part in the Knollwood maneuvers was quite small but that is all I know about it. I rode out to Laurinburg-Maxton Airport near Maxton, North Carolina in a truckload of signal men. We were loaded in alphabetical order. In my glider were Hoyt riding the right hand seat as copilot, Imrich, Heltso, Johnson, Kitchen, and others. We loaded onto a glider one truckload to a glider, the ropes were attached, the engines were running up, the dust was flying. Inside the glider we were engaging in "gallows humor." I asked Heltso what kind of flowers he wanted for his funeral, and he responded to me in kind, when here comes two radio platoon men with a cart load of radio gear. They tied it down to D-rings in the floor right in front of my feet.

I was trying to figure out where to put my feet, as I knew I could not put them on those radio tubes. Captain, or perhaps he was still a Lieutenant, Atwood stuck his nose into the glider and said to me, "You get in that glider over there." He was checking as he always checked, and I am glad he did. He was a good officer.

I got in that other glider, which contained a jeep, an officer, and a driver. In the back seat was a radio, and on the right fender was a power pack, and the only available empty space was on the left fender, and that is where I sat. I had to lean slightly to the left and to the front as there was a part of the glider where I wanted to put my head. I was not too happy about the arrangement, what with leaving my friends, the seating and so on.

Later, I learned that the glider I got out of had crashed, and that my friend Heltso was dead along with another man. Hoyt was injured that night and left the division. I did not see him again until I was on Leyte.

I was not at all proud of my talk in that glider.

Of course more than one glider crashed that night. But I only know of one incident other than the one Heltso was in. My buddy Art was on a glider that landed fast. The impact and momentum unlatched the nose of the glider so that it swung up into the unload position, and Art fell half way out. His legs were under the glider, and he did not want to let go and fall under the thing going at fifty or more miles per hour. He was not strong enough to pull himself up into the glider against all the forces that were acting, and he knew that just as soon as the glider slowed enough the nose would come crashing down and cut him in two. We had some radio gear packed in steel boxes, and just at the last instant one of those boxes fell beside Art when the nose came down. The box was thicker than Art was and he did not get a scratch. God is in control and sometimes he acts on behalf of people.

The glider that I was in made its flight out over the ocean and came back as part of the "invading force" that attacked America that night. I had learned where my drop zone was to be, which happened to be the farm where my wife had once rented a room, and I had walked all over the farm. There was a cotton field, a tobacco field, and a cornfield, and over in the corner were two stone silos. I sure wanted to stay away from them. Across the creek was a pine forest. As we came as if for our landing, I heard something very loud striking the belly of the glider. I could not see out the front of the glider and I felt sure we had overshot and were coming down in the pine forest. I did not think that corn could make so much noise.

But, we made a nice landing in the corn field, and I got out right next to a glider that had two men on top of it with axes. I heard the pilot expressing with much feeling, "I put this overloaded glider in here without a scratch and you are not going to chop the wings off of it." Lt. Atwood turned and pointed and said, "Henry Stimson don't seem to mind." I turned and looked and saw a staff car and three men in overcoats. I presumed one of them was indeed the secretary of war under President Franklin D. Roosevelt.

The reason for chopping off the wings was that that glider contained a big radio, I think it was called the SCR-299, which was normally mounted in a six by six truck with a trailer behind containing a generator to furnish power for it. There is no way you can put a six by six in a glider, so the next best thing was done. The radio was mounted in the glider, and it constituted a full load. There is only one picture of it that I know of. That is found in the paperback book that was published about the time we left Camp Mackall; the cover looks straight up at planes dropping paratroopers and other planes towing gliders. In the Signal Company section is a picture of the glider with the nose either removed or raised, and the operator is wearing an overcoat sitting at the keyboard. It is Ray Ellis.

Up on top of the glider were two Oregon men, wheat rancher Orvile Matheny and logger Richard LaChance. The axes were swinging and the chips were flying. Soon the wings were on the ground and the guys picked up the tail of the glider and set it on the back of a jeep so it could tow the glider backwards on its own wheels. Presto: A working and mobile radio on the ground in the assigned area of the signal corps. I don't know what Henry Stimson thought of it, but I think it was good airborne thinking, taking what you have and making it do what you must do.

My personal job was in the message center; we set up in shelter halves and soon had communications going with division headquarters and with field units. Before long, we got the word that one of our infantry units had been overrun and that the enemy now had all of our code books. We did not truly have anything very complicated at that time. It became my job to sit there all night and make new code books for the entire division. I sat on the ground with a flashlight making new code books with a pencil for each unit. There had to be one for each of the infantry and each of the artillery, all the others, the military police, medics, quartermaster, ordinance, everybody. I finished just as the sun was coming up the next morning. I doubt if anybody could read them in my writing with a pencil, but I made them.

The fact that the Knollwood maneuvers were declared a success caused the U.S. to go ahead with the airborne concept. I knew nothing of the high ranking Americans who were watching us at that time, and I expect that very few others knew either, but without knowing it we made history that day. And, we kept alive the airborne concept. My part in those maneuvers was pretty small, but when all of the parts are put together it was a good operation.

A side-note to the Knollwood Maneuvers:
My wife was living in a house about two hundred yards from the cornfield in which I landed, and she stood out in the road and heard and watched the gliders come in knowing that I was in one of them.

We have been married almost seventy two years now. We still have pretty good health and God has been good to us in wartime and later in peace.

William C. Kitchen

Japanese Jump on San Pablo Airstrip
by William Kitchen

Memory of December 7, 1944

We moved inland from Bito Beach and set up the division headquarters near San Pablo airstrip. We were still living in shelter halves but Division Headquarters was established in a plantation house with the Division Message Center in some sort of a shed very close by. There were at least two message center teams, each capable of operating the message center. I was the cryptographer for one of these teams.

One day, it seems to me that it must have been about the 6th of December, 1944, I received a message in clear text from within Division Headquarters with instructions to send it out to *all units*. The message stated that a Japanese pilot had been shot down, and that in his pocket was a document saying that there was going to be an attack on American forces to take place on Dec. 7th, the anniversary of the attack on Pearl Harbor. That was a strange message because it was not my job to address messages, but to get them sent after they were addressed. However I took that at face value and was busily writing out the names of all the division units, afraid I might miss one.

I had all the infantry units, the artillery units, and was working on the special forces. Just at this time an officer came in from behind me, reached over my shoulder, and took all the papers that I had. He said, "I will take care of this." I thought that as an officer he probably had a better way to do it. Since I received no more information, I went about my job.

The next day, Bill Rudolph was the cryptographer and I had no assignment. The Signal Company Command Post was in a five man pyramidal tent, and in front of it was a pool of water which no one could get around to enter the command post without stepping in. Captain Mabbatt called to me and asked me if I could drain that water away. I will always remember that he *asked* me instead of ordering me. I looked at it and saw that I could dig a ditch and drain away that water, so I worked on it all day long. At one point I was down hip deep in that mud but I got water flowing just about the time of retreat.[11] We had gotten so settled that we had retreat that evening.

Near by was a grassy area with a hand dug well in it, from which we had been told not to drink, but it was clear and we saw no reason not to bathe in it. I know that it had been some time since a bath was available; there were at least a dozen of us standing there, stark naked, dipping up water with our steel helmets tied onto a rope, lathering up, and then getting more water to rinse off. I was just going back to the well for rinse water, when I and all of us looked up and saw three C-47s. At least that is what we thought they were, coming from the direction of the mountains. We all stood and cheered, because we knew that the troops in the mountains were being supplied by L-4 artillery planes, and that they were in a bad way. So, when we saw these planes we thought that the mountain troops had gained enough ground so that they could be supplied by regular aircraft, and thus were in a better position than they had previously been.

Very much to our surprise, those planes began to strafe the ground ahead of them, *at us*. Then we saw paratroops coming out of them. I forgot entirely about getting rid of the G.I. soap on me, and I quickly put on pants and shoes, but nothing else.

---

[11] When the flag is being raised in the morning, you should stand at attention on the first note of "Reveille" and salute. In the evening "Retreat" is played prior to "To the Colors." ("Colors" refer to the flag of the United States and can also include the unit flag)....You normally face the flag when saluting, unless duty requires you to face in some other direction. At the conclusion of the music, resume your regular duties. If you are involved in some duty that would be hampered by saluting, you do not need to salute. (From "The Army Study Guide")

About that time an equipment chute came down about fifty feet from where I was, and never having been in combat before it seemed highly important that I do something, not just stand there. So I fired a full clip of fifteen rounds of .30 caliber carbine ammunition into the bundle.[12]

I was not the only signalman there, but most of them were behind me. Others were firing at that thing too. Suddenly, I was feeling guilty about firing a full clip of bullets into what I knew was not a legitimate target, when a real one might come around the corner at any moment.[13] I also knew Sergeant Bob Main was behind me, as I had just seen him there.

I felt something hit me in the left shoulder and half spin me around. I thought Bob must have thrown a rock at me to tell me to quit wasting my ammunition and to save it for a more needed use later.

Looking around I saw no one, and began to move back to where the rest of the guys were. As I tried to reload I was shaking so that I had trouble reloading my carbine. Several moments later I found that my left shoe was wet, and I wondered why as I had not stepped in any water. I looked down and saw that the shoe was full of red stuff. Stupidly I stared until I realized it was blood. I'd been hit. No pain, none whatsoever after the feeling of being hit by a rock.

I then realized that somebody had fired a round into me.

---

[12] It turned out that it contained hand grenades and small arms ammunition.

[13] Virgil Adamson, an ex-infantry man and smarter than I was, slit the bundle open with his trench knife, and carried it all over to the stream and dumped it into a deep spot. He then wrapped the chute around a rock and threw it in too so that it could not be seen. I don't think that the Japs ever got that stuff.

A medic was walking by, so I approached him and he put some sulfa powder on my wound, and then a triangle bandage on it.[14]

Captain Mabbatt told me to go to the aid station, across the road, which I did. There, I was sent to the back part of the shelter and told to lay down. I didn't sleep much because I could hear the medics working on seriously wounded troops all night. The Japanese did occupy the air strip that night.

The next morning, I saw General Swing lead out a platoon, and they were part of the force that retook the strip. More troops came from other directions to help in retaking the strip. I laid around most of the day, and about dark they loaded a bunch of us onto an ambulance, and we started on the trip to the coast and to a hospital.

The rest is history. The raid was short as far as I was concerned. It was a total surprise to me, even though I had personally processed the message about it. I had expected the raid to be on other people, not on me.

Fifty years later I read in *The Voice*[15] General Muller's story called *Listen As You Have Never Listened Before*, and about the message he tried to send and how General Swing had pulled the message because he thought the Japs did not have the ability to pull off a significant raid.

I may be wrong, but I believe that I was on the edge of that story by General Muller. I know now that the Japanese were not interested in 11th Airborne Division Headquarters. They were interested in the L-4 planes and in the supplies they carried that were making a difference up in the mountains. Yes, they would have liked to have the airstrip, but they did not have the ability to take and hold it, so they concentrated on destroying supplies and aircraft.

---

[14] For a full account of my being wounded, please see the chapter entitled "Personal Remembrances"

[15] *The Voice of the Angels*, the 11th Airborne newspaper, is published quarterly.

They destroyed a lot of stuff that night, but due to the war effort at home there was a lot more available to us, so the setback was not a really serious setback to our war effort.

The guys in the mountains were already on short rations. It was worse for them for awhile, but they hung in there and eventually succeeded in driving the Japs out of the mountains.[16] As always the infantry are the guys that get the job done. My hat is off to them.

These are my memories of the San Pablo Airstrip drop by the Japanese army.[17]

William C. Kitchen, 511th Airborne Signal Company

---

[16] Mountains run north to south the entire length of Leyte.

[17] Most of the author's letters home still exist, though the ones Marge wrote to him have been destroyed.

Bob LeRoy ~ In the Mountains

This story has been copied from the gospel tract that was prepared by Bob LeRoy, a trooper with the 511ᵗʰ Parachute infantry, part of the 11ᵗʰ Airborne Division in WWII. It is a first person account of what our men were doing in the mountains of Leyte in 1944. Bob LeRoy later became a traveling evangelist.

Christmas in Combat – The Christmas I'll Never Forget

For several weeks our Parachute Battalion had hunted the enemy through the dense jungles on the island of Leyte. Slipping over moss covered logs, wading swift rivers, and forging new trails, we marched and fought our way, fifteen miles clear across this Japanese controlled island. From a great distance we could have appeared as a long column of "winding worker ants," rather than a Battalion of American soldiers. Our packs were always heavy with the military necessities of our life. Our feet were usually tired and sore, as we marched continually forward through the wet tropical underbrush, each hour we rested during a ten minute break. Every ounce of strength was needed for this "human hunt" in which we were all engaged. Yes, it was a most dangerous game, for the prey was cunning, ruthless and very well trained for this type of warfare. Our orders were "cut off all enemy supply lines and take no prisoners." At night we always took turns sleeping, and then standing a lonely guard beside our faithful cold black machine guns. They had proved to be the best protection against the enemy.

We Captured Rock Hill

December 5th, 1944 found our lone battalion, (one third of the 511ᵗʰ Parachute Infantry Regiment) in a most precarious position, militarily speaking. We had fought our way inland only about eight miles, to the foot of a mountain around 7,000 feet high. Here we crossed over and captured a large section of the Japanese major supply trail, their only lifeline to the coast. This was accomplished with loss of life on both sides. One of my best friends was killed during this first contact with the enemy. When found later during a quiet hour, his body had been ransacked and his boots were missing. The enemy was vicious and outnumbered us eight to one.

We had no choice, except to climb on up to the mountain and "dig in." We were ready for battle within the hour. Viewed from a distance, this jungle covered mountain top resembled a huge loaf of French bread. It had steep sides, but more gradual slopes at each end. Our machine gun positions were about 100 yards apart, with riflemen stationed in foxholes every ten steps apart. The entire camp covered the top of the mountain, with the medics, Battalion Commander, and Communication staff stationed near the center of the huge oval.

Our Food All Gone

Two days passed. There was still no counterattack so we waited and waited. Far removed from any reinforcements, surrounded by the enemy, with food all gone, we were facing certain death. Sagely our commander said, "We have the Japs just where they want us." A sudden change in the weather had also contributed to our dilemma. The rainy season had descended upon us without warning, thus cutting off our entire airborne supply line. At the start of this campaign, cargo planes called "biscuit bombers" had dropped supplies to us about twice each week. But now there was a great blanket of dark clouds totally obscuring our position from their view. Two weeks had passed since our last food supply had been dropped. Even then, one of our men had been killed by a swift falling fifty pound K-ration box. However those rations were all gone now and I had just divided my last small tin of cheese into six even, small pieces – one piece for every man in my squad, and one left over that was given to the Battalion Commander, who happened to be walking by at just the right time. I had saved this tin of cheese for several days to be used as a final source of energy. I decided to share it on that day.

Lost Battalion of WWII

Christmas was now only ten days away. We had received no mail since Thanksgiving. We were another "lost Battalion" of WWII, deserted by all except the enemy. The warm tropical rain pattered down relentlessly upon the large banana leaves that dangled just above my head. It seemed that nearly everything only added to our mental and physical discomfort. Only a miracle could save us from these bitter circumstances. Gradually my spiritual eyes turned toward the great Creator who alone could help us. My *thoughts went back to the time when I was a boy of twelve. It was then, during a special meeting at our church, that I allowed Christ to enter into my life. Since that day I had always tried my best to trust God completely for all of my spiritual and earthly needs. I fully believed that he would not fail me now.*

Best to Die Fighting

We were anxious for battle, for we thought it better to die fighting than from slow starvation. The enemy seemed to know that our food was gone and our morale was very low. They were waiting for the psychological time to strike, and we knew it. It happened on December the sixteenth, in the evening. I was suddenly startled by a bullet that tore a slender branch from the tree that was right above me. Rifle fire from our men quickly followed, and then the enemy swarmed toward us. The nips came screaming, yelling and shooting from all directions. The battle raged at both ends of the camp simultaneously, but again our faithful machine guns took their toll. The shooting was actually over in less than 20 minutes, with the Japanese loss very heavy, as usual, compared to our own. We slept none that night.

Banzai after Banzai

The next two days followed in the same pattern with two banzai attacks daily, one at sunrise and one at sunset. Although we won each battle, we were getting weaker by the day from hunger. From the slain Japanese nearest us, we would take what few grains of dried beans or rice we could find. This was done only to prolong our lives. On December 18th I tried to climb out of my two foot foxhole, but an invisible hand seemed to push me back. I fell to the ground in a semi-conscious state. When I revived about an hour later, I felt as though I had been asleep for a long time. Realizing that my body had gone without food — one handful of rice in over one week — it is no wonder I had fainted under the strain of those unforgettable days.

My Foxhole Prayer

Under my raincoat shelter that day, I breathed a prayer. "Please Dear God, give us all more strength to help us win this war for thee, and for our country, that someday we may once again worship you in peace and happiness. I ask this in my Savior's

name. Amen." I somehow felt stronger after this. My spirit was
revived and some of my strength returned. Slowly I crawled
toward my steel helmet, which was being used to catch rainwater
that dripped from my shelter roof. After drinking several swallows
I felt even more revived. This day had been quiet with no fighting
at all and we surely needed the rest. It was the morning of
December 19th. I was rudely awakened by my sergeant. He said,
"You're needed for grave detail right now." This meant that some
of the men in my company had died during the night. In our
present condition it took all six men to carry the body of one dead
American to his grave. We sometimes placed three or four bodies in
one grave, simply because we did not have the strength to dig
individual graves, for the roots were thick and the mud was heavy.
At this particular burial we used the last of our supply parachutes
to wrap the bodies of our comrades. To us the "chutes" were the
only remaining symbols of the fighting spirit for which those men
had been noted.

If I Die, Who'll Tell Mom?

At Div. HQ the word went out that the Chaplain had showed
up at the air field with his parachute and the General said, "The
Chaplain don't have to go there." To which the Chaplain replied
"That's where the Chaplain is needed."

After the solemn "ashes to ashes, dust to dust" service I got to
thinking again as I slowly staggered back toward my foxhole.
"How will my family ever know what became of me if we all die up
here on this mountain top?" At this very moment I was given a
friendly greeting from the chaplain's assistant. "All of you men
who believe in God and the Holy Bible are invited to meet for
prayer at noon today."

Life's Greatest Meeting

This was one of the most important and strangest invitations I
had ever received in my life. For us rough and tough paratroopers,
it was unheard of to actually be invited to an official U.S. Army
prayer meeting, let alone ever actually attend one! Again my
thoughts went back to my childhood in Tacoma, Washington,
where I had somehow learned the words that Jesus spoke to his
followers: "I will never leave thee nor forsake thee." Now my heart

seemed to beat with a new hope, for I thought that with God's help, certainly all things are possible. With this assurance in my heart, I personally invited several other men in my company to attend with me. It was the most unusual meeting I have ever witnessed in my life.

LeRoy the Religious Nut

Some of these men who in years past had referred to me as "a sort of religious crackpot" failed to joke with me now, as I approached the various foxholes with my odd invitation. The men would usually nod their heads in approval and promise to be there. Others would pretend to not hear, and would continue on cleaning their rifles or smoking their last cigarettes. At first I was disappointed while attending this meeting. For only about a dozen men out of the camp of about three hundred were present. While waiting for the service to begin, the words of Jesus again came to my mind: "Where two or three are gathered together in my name, there I am in the midst of them." Our Chaplain stood before us, undaunted in spirit; he suggested that we each silently ask God's forgiveness for our sins. I had never experienced a service like this before. Then followed a reading from scriptures by Lee Walker, Chaplain. When he finished he said "Now men, we are ready to ask for supernatural help from God. Let us all pray."

God Hears Our Cries

We became soldiers of another kingdom as we dropped to our knees in the mud. Yes we were humble before our heavenly father, indifferent now to the rain that fell on our bare heads. It only helped wash away some of the dirt and tears from our bearded faces, uplifted towards God's heaven. Our hearts were in touch with our maker. Our spirits cried out for divine guidance, strength and final deliverance from this bloody hill which we named "Rock Hill" after our Regimental Commander Rock Haugen. Again I returned to my foxhole wet, tired and weak, but still hopeful. I glanced casually across the sky at the dark clouds overhead; they seemed like giant vultures, slowly circling their prey.

Then my eyes came to rest on a spot in the sky. It grew lighter by the minute! My head grew dizzy from the strain of my eyes and neck. I sank down onto a weather-beaten old log, still gazing upward. Suddenly, like the shutters of a gigantic telescope being pulled back, the clouds began to open, the sunshine came through a beautiful clear blue porthole in a ceiling of total darkness.

The Sky Opens Wide

Excitement was in the air as everyone began to watch the opening in the sky, looking and watching, yet almost unwilling to believe their eyes as the sun shone through. The minutes went by; suddenly there appeared a tiny black speck in the bright blue opening! Down, down it came towards us, as if a mighty eagle swooping to feed her young. The shout rang out, "A biscuit bomber is overhead! Heads up!" What an occasion to remember! The old C-47 dropping us supplies at every pass over this rugged mountain top battle ground. To us it was manna from heaven. After a goodbye dip of her majestic wings, she circled higher and higher up through the opening and out of sight. God had heard and answered the prayers of his children that December week of 1944. We now had rations, but some ate too much. This bulky food in our dry, shrunken stomachs resulted in nausea and vomiting for several of us. The next day, Christmas, we felt better. The order came to move off the mountain at all cost. Our two rifle companies took the lead. That morning we completely surprised the enemy soldiers camped just below us. They scattered in wild disorder and those that remained were soon killed. One Japanese fell dead across the trail in front of me; since my belt had been broken and I needed one badly, I took his. I later brought it home to the states where it now hangs on the wall of my study. By noon that blessed Christmas Day we had fought another small battle in the lower foothills on our rapid drive to the coast, now just a few miles away. That afternoon brought us

---

Trouble in the Mountains

A note here by W. C. Kitchen:

I was at division headquarters at this time. We knew of the trouble in the mountains but couldn't help them. The story went around headquarters that Chaplain Walker showed up at the airstrip with his parachute and that General Swing told him, "The chaplain doesn't have to go up there." To which Chaplain Walker replied, "That's where the chaplain is needed." Forty five years later at a reunion several men approached Chaplain Walker and quoted for him the scripture which he read that day. They loved him.

our final victory against the enemy. Thus ended the conquest of Leyte.

I Dreamed of Home.

Only a person who has spent many days or weeks in the dark tropical jungle can fully appreciate what a wonderful Christmas present this day of victory turned out to be. Even our wounded comrades who were being carried from our shoulders on makeshift stretchers smiled or joked to one another in spite of their suffering. We were happy. Our commander had given us orders to "rest up for one week at the ocean beach." Finally, it stopped raining and by the time we reached the ocean shore the ground was dry and warm. What a thrill it was to drop my packs and weapons, take off my boots and worn out socks, then slide my aching feet into the warm ocean sand. With my worn out but faithful army pack tucked under my head, I soon found myself falling asleep. I dreamed of home, and thanked my dear Lord for giving me such a wonderful present as this — His own birthday.

Lord God of Hosts, be with us lest we forget, lest we forget.

An Airborne Soldier's Prayer

O loving God, Creator and Sustainer of life: I am grateful that You have permitted me to live into the autumn of life. I remember the old days when I was one of the young, the strong and the brave. Even then You were the medicine for our fears. You were the wind beneath our wings.

Do for me now, O God, what I cannot do for myself. When sickness and pain come as an unwelcome guest to me, or to someone I love; or the skies turn gray because I can't do everything I once did; or sorrow knocks at my door; or taps are sounded for a loved one or an old trooper friend; or when I grow impatient and discouraged with myself and the world, then O God...

Save me from the inertia of futility.

Remind me how You answered my prayers in combat, when I was alone and afraid.

Grant that my trust level may be as high now as it was then.

Give me the power of Your Spirit that I may be strong again.

Put a guard detail around my loneliness, reminding me that there are loyal friends and airborne buddies near and far who still remember and care.

Give me the faith to live one day at a time.

Create in me an unfaltering faith in an unfailing God.

And grant me the light to see beyond the present, no matter how dark it may be, and into the Great Forever.

For Yours is the Kingdom, and the Power, and the Glory. And I am Yours.

In Your Holy Name, Amen.

Lee Edwin Walker

Harold *Spring* and Dr. Tom Nestor

The Story of Harold Spring
F Company, 511th Airborne Signal Company
One Soldier's Will to Live
Rewritten by George Doherty. First reported in Airborne
Quarterly *by Ralph Ermantinger*

*On 5 December 1944 while traversing a mountain trail in
heavy jungle on Leyte Island in the Philippines, a Japanese
machine gunner in an ambush situation fired a burst of hot bullets
into the belly of Corporal Harold Spring that almost cut him in
two. Now it must be said that in almost any case where a similar
situation took place, the initial shock of the burst would kill the
victim almost immediately. Not Harold Spring. Now I could have
waited until the last page of this story to tell you that he, in fact,
survived the torture from the wound and is alive fifty years later.
Why did he survive? How did he survive? How, why, where, when
and what happened? Witnesses to the ambush said Spring died in
the gunfire that ensued.*

*Spring fell so close to the enemy machine gunner, who was
lying in wait for a recovery team, ready to give them a burst of
Spring's medicine that Captain Charles Morgan, the Company
Commander of F Company decided not to attempt a recovery at
that time. Two of Harold's friends, Ernie Koop and Louis Vane,
asked Captain Morgan permission to try. That was a heroic
request on their part. They made their plan to crawl in close on
their bellies, make a quick dash to Spring and pull his body into the
heavy jungle lining the trail, which would afford them some cover
and concealment. They were successful in retrieving Spring, not
knowing at that time whether they had rescued a corpse or a live
buddy. As you know he was still alive.*

*After dragging and pulling him in that very scary situation
they finally reached a point where medics could check his
bedraggled and badly wounded body. Happily they announced he
was still alive but unconscious from the shock and loss of blood.
Captain Morgan ordered a team to make a makeshift litter from a*

poncho and two bamboo poles and head back to the battalion aid station where Captain Thomas Nestor, M.D. waited.

Dr. Nestor didn't waste any time passing the time of day with the survivors. He sprang into action. Immediately after surveying Springs wounds he sent one man down the hill to fetch a helmet full of water from the creek, and directed other medics to strip off Spring's clothing – or what there was left of it. He ordered a small trench dug and made ready his instruments. Now get this scenario: Spring was laid out on that muddy hilltop in a trench probably filled with bacteria and microbes. Critters you and I wouldn't want crawling around our bodies in the best of circumstances, let alone where they could feast on Spring's open wounds. It was a perfect invitation to disaster and infection. All the guidelines for safe sterilization were forsaken because there just wasn't any choice. You either worked with what you had or you didn't work, knowing the final result could be death. Infection in the jungle was something every wounded man dreaded, as did the healthy troops.

Captain Nestor performed a miracle in that slit trench, using instruments that for all practical purposes were non-sterilized and with nothing but ether for an anesthetic, and the Lord performed another one. This was only one of many such miracles in the jungles of Leyte which this super surgeon performed every day under the most trying of circumstances.

Because of the incessant rain and fading light, as well as the fact that Spring was in deep shock, Captain Nestor had to work very fast. He laid open the abdominal wounds even wider and scooped out the viscera, stitched the little black holes made by the bullets closed, made other repairs while he was in there, and then proceeded to put everything back in place. Then he closed the incisions and the operation was over. Back in the states this would have called for a team of three or four physicians and a half dozen surgical nurses as well as an anesthesiologist.

The soldiers who carried Spring to surgery from the ambush stayed and watched Captain Nestor in action and continued to help in any way they were asked. The surgery appeared to take only a few minutes to perform but obviously was a tedious task under trying and very critical circumstances. There was no tent, no surgical table, no amenities, no surgical procedures to follow in this Godforsaken hellhole. Spring was wrapped in a wet blanket and placed in the trench, which some thought would be his grave, for when Captain Nestor was asked what Spring's chances were, he said, "Not one in a million."

You know what? Spring beat that lottery!! He thwarted the men who came at the first light of day to shovel dirt in his face. They couldn't believe it when they could see there was still life in that body. Dr. Nestor was called to see if they could be mistaken. The disbelieving Nestor said, "There should be doctors for paratroopers and other doctors for ordinary people."

Ralph Ermatinger, of F Company, 511ᵗʰ PI[18], a friend of Spring's, witnessed the surgery in a disbelieving manner after seeing Spring's multiple wounds. He said, "Truly it can be said that Harold's spirit had a fierce muscle in it."

One of the doctors at the jungle hospital later said to Spring that he "wouldn't have given a wooden nickel" for Spring's life when they brought him in. He then showed Spring a wooden cross lying up against a tree, and asked if Spring knew who it was for.

"I guess me," Spring said.

"You're right," the doctor said. Spring didn't know it but a grave had already been dug for him just outside the hut!

In an interview with Spring he related his story. "One morning a young Filipina girl living with her family in a hut at the foot of the hill where the small hospital staff and I were billeted came running up the hill hysterically yelling, "Japanese, Japanese." Just before she reached our hut the Japanese chasing her shot her in the back. I was lying on the floor on a litter when it all started. The yelling and bullets came crashing through the tissue paper thin hut. It was lucky that I was lying on a litter. Had I been standing up the bullets would have surely crashed into my battered body.

---

[18] Parachute Infantry

The water cans were hit and water started spraying out of them. I was tempted to look for a means of taking my own life because I didn't want to give the Japs the satisfaction that they had killed a defenseless American (and it probably would have been in a brutal manner). I knew they did not take prisoners, as we didn't. If I was to die I decided I would die fighting just as I was trained to do. But I couldn't. I obviously didn't have a weapon or the strength to use one. The dilemma itself left me exhausted just thinking about it. I rose up on one elbow and looked out the door. To my horror they were coming straight for the hut. I knew that was it – kaput! Hellfire and damnation, I had to blow the Japs away, but with what? All of a sudden the beautiful sound of a light machine gun started rat-ta-tatting out the beautiful tune of Yankee Doodle Dandy. In my high school yearbook is a notation: Harold Spring joins army and plays Yankee Doodle Dandy on a machine gun for Uncle Sam. Fortunately some of our boys had quickly moved into a position on the flank of the onrushing Japs and cut loose with a machine gun. Yankee Doodle Dandy, you betcha my life, you son of a gun.

During that attack a mortar shell landed in the mud just a few feet from my position in the hut and very close to my head. After the attack, which lasted only a few minutes, was over, the surviving Japs slithered back into the slime and jungles from which they came. I was quickly taken out of the hut so they could detonate the un-spent mortar round.

Departure day from the jungle and parts unknown finally came. I was about to leave F Company, the 511th, and my buddies forever, but not in spirit and will. I knew my combat days were over and the future didn't look too promising, except for getting out of the jungles of Leyte and the eternal rain, leaches and critters (some of which have never been registered either Republican or Democratic).

Manarawat was a small plateau in the middle of the island where the 3rd Battalion of the 511th had hacked down coconut trees and jungle using only machetes to carve a small airstrip that would accommodate L-4s and L-5s.

L-4 Air Ambulance

Piper J-5 Cruisers were used by the U.S. Navy as air ambulances. They were powered by a 100 horsepower engine and called HE-1s. A hinged "turtledeck" fuselage allowed a stretcher to be loaded. (When the Navy realigned their "H" designation for their helicopters, the HE-1 became the *AE-1*.)

From Warbird Alley www.warbirdalley.com

The blowing of stumps and the finished job was accomplished with the direction of engineers from C-Company, 127th Engineers Battalion. They jumped on the clearing to blow stumps and otherwise make the strip serviceable for the small aircraft with which their pilots would land and take off on missions of mercy. Each plane would land with much needed supplies, mostly medical. These supplies were too important to hazard a throw out the door and hope for a safe landing, or even to drop by parachute which too often meant delivery to the Japs. Once they landed and unloaded their precious cargo, a litter case would be strapped under the wing, outside the fuselage, and they would take off headed for Tacloban. Those who could sit in the rear seat would do so. I had to ride outside. It was the thrill of a lifetime.

These pilots as well as the C-47 pilots who dropped supplies to us were unsung heroes. It was especially dangerous when they were making a dive to drop their cargo from just above the tree tops. I'm afraid that most people took it for granted that once the aircraft was airborne it was "Bon Voyage." Not so. This was when they were most vulnerable. We lost several planes to Jap small arms fire this way.

Once I arrived on my L-4 ambulance at Tacloban I was put onto a four wheeled ambulance marked with large red crosses that the Japs refused to recognize. We headed for Dulag where we started from. Not quite though, Bito Beach, south of Dulag was the "real" kicking off point. During the trip to Dulag I heard music, wonderful music, but not a harp I assure you.

Somebody brought me two bananas when I arrived at the 1st Convalescent Hospital on the beach at Dulag. I was so hungry I ate both of them. I was skin and bones by that time. As a matter of fact, I could take either hand, grasp my calf and touch my thumb without any trouble. Now that's skinny!

Once I arrived at the hospital they immediately took me into a large tent with other seriously wounded. They gently put me into a real bed with a mattress, white sheets and a pillow. That was glorious! The trouble was I couldn't sleep. It was too comfortable! I was used to sleeping on the ground with my helmet for a pillow. I must admit I didn't particularly miss that trench or the hut on stilts. It took me a long time before I could get into a deep sleep. I guess it was from sheer exhaustion that I did finally fall to sleep. I remember reliving those horrible hours and days over and over again. It was a great feeling to know that I could lay there without the horrible feeling that some Japs might come crashing in and cut my throat. At that time I hadn't heard of the Japanese paratroopers who had landed only a couple of weeks before all over the territory in which I felt so secure.

I was surprised to find a Hebrew in the bed on my right who prayed all day in Hebrew, which was very

Pilipino

On December 13, 1937, President Manuel L. Quezon issued an executive order approving the adoption of Tagalog as the basis of the national language of the Philippines. In 1959, the language became known as *Pilipino* in an effort to distinguish it from the Tagalog ethnic group. Later study has linked Tagalog, Filipino, and Pilipino as essentially one language, which is where the issue stands today.

Filipino is constitutionally designated as the national language of the Philippines and is, along with English, one of two official languages.

From Wikipedia, the Free Encyclopedia

educational in a way. In the bed on my left was a Pilipino boy with part of his face missing.

As any boy would, he was playing soldier with a grenade he found, not really knowing how lethal and deadly his toy was. His pretty little sister came to visit him every day. Because I was without stomach muscles, I discovered that without them it was difficult to talk. Therefore I didn't talk too much with them. I will say it felt good to see a civilian again. Especially when just a couple of days before I had thought I never again would.

A young soldier behind me had been shot in the head. Day and night he kept saying, "If I'm a good boy may I go home now, please?" After a couple of days they moved me to where I do not know. It might have been the same hospital and just another tent or a completely different hospital. I know not where. Ta Da! When the ambulance door was opened I saw a man from my home town of Lansing, Michigan by the name of Robert Forbes. Little did I know it would turn out to be such a blessing. I was starved. Bob sold my Zippo lighter and bought or traded it for some candy bars. I hid the candy from the moochers and boy did I have a feast!

One day a medic came into our ward and told us to prepare to leave by packing whatever we had in the way of personal items, because they were moving us out to a hospital ship. We were carried aboard a small landing craft in rows of stretchers manned by the Navy. After we arrived alongside the great white hospital ship U.S.S. Hope (a ship of mercy with red crosses painted on her side) I was hoisted by boom and crane and taken immediately to a ward below. The problem was that all the beds were taken and I was still in too serious a condition to be left on a folding cot. A sailor who overheard my plight offered his bed to me, which the medical corps gratefully accepted. It was a bed with a firm mattress and white sheets as well as an overhead light. Back in Leyte as soon as it got dark outside it got dark inside.

They didn't have any lights except the one which the medics carried when making their rounds checking each patient.

A medical officer came by to check each of the new patients and grant their wishes if possible. I was asked if I was hungry.

"Yes, sir" I said with a wide grin.

He said, "Spring, you can have anything you want to eat." He turned to a member of the ship's medical staff and said, "Make sure he gets it." Then he turned to me and said "Your body is using your muscle tissue to keep you alive. I have some plasma if you want it."

I said, "Yes sir!"

U.S.S. Hope

The USS *Hope* was a *Comfort*-class hospital ship launched on August 30th, 1943 and commissioned as a Navy hospital ship on August 15th, 1944. *Hope* was one of three hospital ships built, commanded and crewed by the U.S. Navy for the Army. These ships, unlike the Navy hospital ships, were intended for the evacuation and transport of patients after primary care had been given. Medical equipment and personnel were provided by the Army. *Hope* arrived in Leyte Gulf on November 7th, 1944 to care for casualties and evacuate them. Thereafter the ship made four more voyages to Leyte to evacuate wounded. *Hope* sailed on April 9th, 1945 to take part in the Okinawa operation, arriving off the island four days later. She sailed

 on October 22nd with returnees, arriving in San Francisco on November 15th, and subsequently made two more voyages to Guam and the Philippines to bring back the sick and wounded. The *U.S.S. Hope* was decommissioned May 9th, 1946.

Beds and patients were shuffled around so that all the seriously wounded got a good surgical bed. I was put in a bed next to a surgical table where the wounded were treated. Gangrenous and wounded flesh was discharged into a bucket near my head but by that time I didn't care. I knew by that time they were putting distance between the ship and the Philippines. While I was there I watched a steady stream of seriously wounded soldiers placed on the surgical table and treated or operated on for their wounds. Some didn't make it. A young interested sailor would talk to me during the serious ones, which gave me comfort. The nurses were kind to me also, as they were to all the badly wounded. When we crossed the equator I knew it, for it was stifling hot below decks and I couldn't do anything about it. Unlike the Sea Pike, when the 511th crossed over the equator there were no King Neptune festivities that I heard of.

After what seemed an awful long time, the U.S.S. Hope anchored at Hollandia in New Guinea. I think it was either Christmas Eve or New Year's Eve. At any rate no one on shore was too happy to see the hospital ship arrive, for it meant continuous work by the shore crew until all were safely ashore and in the hospital. Shortly after arriving, a medical doctor making the rounds stopped by my bed and lifted the loose bandage covering my wounds, only to drop it on the floor. After picking it up he shook loose any dirt that accumulated on the bandage and proceeded to place it back on the exposed wound. The officer had obviously been drinking jungle-juice I guess. I worried all night about the incident and was concerned about infection, although what I had just been through was much worse than the dirty bandage. Infection was unlikely, I thought. After a couple of days my eyes and throat started to fester and ache. The ward doctor told me I had a strep or staph infection. I said "Oh, noo!" My father had died of strep in 1937. The doctor gave me sulfa drugs and my wounds were bathed in a penicillin solution each day. Penicillin was relatively new and the hospital staff wasn't too sure how it worked, if at all.

The hospital overlooked an airbase, so each day I would watch the A-20s take off to bomb isolated pockets of Jap stragglers. This helped take my mind off my own troubles for awhile. With my mind running wild, it became a game of imagining what was happening on the receiving end of the attack bombers. This was stimulating and relaxing, a mind game for the body.

After what seemed like forever, the day came when they told us we were going home. "Going home! Yippie woooow!! Just too much!!" It was overwhelming. The thought of going home to the states was the happiest day of my life. A day I wasn't sure I would live to see a few weeks earlier.

We stopped at Guadalcanal for a short time to refuel and then headed for Tarawa where I thought of all the Marines who gave their lives and bodies for that small piece of real estate. It was just another stepping stone on the way home. There were psychos aboard the plane which didn't make the trip any easier.

"You think I'm crazy, don't you?" one fellow said.

I replied "No, why should I?"

He said he had fought in several battles and knew his time was up. Not wanting to go home in a basket he grabbed an officer by the throat and said "I'll kill you, you...Jap." They grabbed him and there he was on that plane. He said, "I hate to go home this way, but it's still better than in a basket."

I'm not sure about that. He will have to live with that decision the rest of his life.

I hadn't walked since being wounded, but on that flight I crawled out of my litter with help and walked to the latrine. Wow was that great! Just to feel a little normal again. You can't imagine how exciting that was.

After a couple more refueling stops, the plane landed in Hawaii. Seeing all that greenery and signs in English was

almost too much to bear without breaking down. It was like
the pearly gates and seeing heaven. You knew there was no
war here, even though it all started here. Green grass,
sidewalks, paved streets and street lights. Yep, I felt the same
way some of you are feeling right now as your mind tries to
sort out what it must have been like for someone who was
told he was dead. The plane's door opened and in came
beautiful people; civilians with beautiful clean clothes. They
looked so happy. Big smiles, lipstick and all that good stuff
that went with it. I found out that my sailor brother had just
shipped out the week before from Pearl Harbor. How
disappointing!

The stay in Hawaii was short. We headed for California
and all I could think of was that great song, "California Here
We Come." Finally it was time. We had made it! I felt the
wheels of the great bird thump on the tarmac, and then the
runway. Home at last. How can I express my feeling? With a
few tears I guess, but that wouldn't be dignified for a
paratrooper to do, would it? Ah, I'll just do it privately – for
the guys still over there. For them there would be no more
"over theres."

Emotional? You bet it was. You never appreciate
America until you don't have that old mother any longer. I
guess that's why we get so upset when we see activists
demonstrating against the guy in the billboard with the
goatee pointing at you and saying, "I want you." Dear God,
you made America great, adorable, lovable, and blessed with
great people. I just want to reach out and hug her. It's great
to be home, America!

As I departed from the plane, I noticed newsreel
cameras were recording the event and several reporters were
interviewing the wounded. They were loaded into
ambulances and some in buses to be taken to a nearby
hospital. Wouldn't you know that a snafu had to take place
right off the bat? I was taken to a V.D. ward by mistake
where no one was smiling. A soldier said very sternly, "We
are having an inspection today. You will have to make your

bed and stand at attention." I was bewildered by this order. First I couldn't stand if I wanted to and second, I thought, "Is this the way they treat seriously wounded soldiers?" Not knowing the others had wounds but not by the enemy. Not me! When the inspecting officers arrived one of them asked "What's wrong with you soldier?"

I replied, "I have an abdominal wound sir."

Shock came over the officer's face. He read the medical wounded record hanging at the end of the bed and with a snap to he ordered the orderlies, "Get this wounded soldier upstairs where he belongs." He apologized to me and went about his business.

They took me upstairs and what a difference it made. Here were my war buddies. No arms, no legs but all with laughing faces when they heard my story. They started cutting up and jockeying the nurses like a bunch of teenagers – which some of them still were. The nurses, of course, took it all in stride and good-naturedly. They were happy for me too. What we were in was a "holding pen" until the administrative staff could work out the details to send all of us to the specialty hospital nearest to our homes. We knew that for most of us, this would be the last time we would be together. We had come a long way since the hospital ship Hope and Leyte. I must say that it was sad to see them leave in ones and twos and sometimes in threes and fours. As for me, I was destined for Chicago and the hospital.

While flying over the Rockies in Colorado we started bucking impossible headwinds and had to turn back to the nearest airport. We were taken to the nearest hospital where we were wined and dined and entertained by a bunch of college girls who came out to visit us. One did a strip dance and I must say that most of the GIs turned their heads in embarrassment. You must remember this was 1945 and although we had fought a war we were still naïve when it came to women.

When we finally got the go ahead to travel, we arrived in Chicago and the hospital about 2:00 a.m. I was left in a hallway on a stretcher. You could say, "What else is new?" I had seen more of a stretcher that last month than any bed. After a while I got a little lonesome when I realized that everyone else had gone home and forgotten me. I decided to go to Ward 5I-A on the fifth floor where I had been assigned. I rolled off the stretcher, gathered my knees under me and slowly stood up. I could only take small steps because the muscles in my abdomen gave way reluctantly and it was sheer torture. My stomach felt like it had a huge stone in it. Slowly I made it some hours later.

I told the ward orderly who I was and what happened. He assigned me to a bed. A few minutes later he came to me just as I was ready to crawl into bed and said, "The ward officer wanted me to report to his office. I was sure it wasn't to pin any medals on me for my heroic effort or to apologize to me for leaving me in the hall downstairs. When I arrived he took my bandages off and asked what happened? When I told him the whole story he looked at me with an incredulous eye and said, "You don't really expect me to believe that cock and bull do you?" I answered, "When an officer in my outfit asks you a question you answer him forthrightly and with the truth." He asked me what I thought of the officers here in the states and I answered the only way I could by saying, "I haven't been here long enough to have an opinion. I do know the ones over there are the best of the best." He took it as a personal affront and told me to go back to my bunk. From then on he gave me trouble.

I had to walk to the first floor to get my meals. For some "mysterious" reason it wasn't written on my bed chart that I was a bed patient. They might have done me a favor inadvertently by forcing me to walk much earlier than was normal in those days.

One of the nurses who took a liking to me or felt sorry for me or both, asked me if I wanted to work in the ward office. I said sure, knowing that staying busy would be better than laying in bed feeling sorry for myself. I delivered charts and blood samples and did many other small jobs whenever they needed me and weren't in a rush.

After a while GIs who had been prisoners in Germany started arriving. Some were in pitiful shape, others like they had never spent a day in a German prison. They had everything from frost bite to chiggers. The ones from the Pacific and Japanese Prisoner of War Camps were tragic cases and tore at your heart strings. They were emaciated, skinny as a rail with gaunt looking faces and eyes bulging, almost too much to believe. They were unsmiling, like zombies, so sad, so terribly sad.

I kept thinking of my buddies I left on Leyte who were now on Luzon, wondering how they were doing. I scanned the papers every day to no avail. It seemed the 11th was forgotten or just wasn't written about. All the other divisions seemed to get more than their share of ink. I wanted to write but I couldn't – mostly for obvious reasons such as moving constantly from one hospital to another, too weak, no paper, no pen or pencil. The usual excuses you understand, but the truth. Hollywood would have had a beautiful woman riding with me, writing my letters for me. No such luck for this GI.

Several years after the war I got my Purple Heart when it was least expected, but greatly appreciated. The 11th Airborne Division sent me a Japanese Samurai sword as a memento and as a way of saying thanks. Nice, huh? My billfold caught up to me two years after I was wounded; the important thing was it did get to me.

It wasn't the contents, but the meaning. Thanks to all you guys who could so easily have walked off with it.

The doctor who performed my skin grafts took great pride in his work. He created a new gauze which when removed would not stick to the body, or pull open old wounds. I was told not to lift my head after surgery and was given no reason except that I would be very sorry if I did.

When I came out of recovery all I could think about was liquids. A nurse said, "Here is some orange juice, drink it." Now think of this, you're laying flat on your back right? How are you going to drink a glass of orange juice, even with a straw? You can't. So I rose up to gulp it down, thinking if I did it fast it would be okay, right? No, not alright. I passed out. For three days I was out of it. I had jaundice and that ain't good. I sweated so much the nurses said they had to change my pajamas twice, and I had to be unconscious, wouldn't you know it?

Afterword

Harold Spring was discharged from the Army in May of 1945 when he returned to Michigan to begin life anew as a civilian. He and his new bride, Belle Enberg, successfully raised her three children and two beautiful children they propagated and are very happy to this day.

We give medals to those fearless fighters who did something extraordinary under difficult circumstances. How about Captain Tom Nestor, M.D.? Didn't he perform his duties under incredibly difficult circumstances without the proper tools to perform his emergency surgery, seven days a week at any hour, not just from 8:00 a.m. to 5:00 p.m.? How about his male nurses (medics)? It had to be very trying on them also.

Captain Tom Nestor, M.D. died November, 1992 at his home in Wakefield, Rhode Island, remembered only by those whose lives he saved or put back together again.

I am just as guilty as everyone else. I'm afraid I took the medics and the medical doctors for granted without giving them their just due. From all that I have been reading and hearing about Dr. Tom Nestor, this is probably the way he would have wanted it anyway. No fanfare, no public recognition. He knew in his heart that those soldiers whom he performed his miracles on remember. **They loved him and he loved them.** *I don't remember ever coming in contact with you, Dr. Tom, but I promise you I'll never forget you.*

Second Island Luzon
Corporal Lynn

One Day in the Life of Corporal Lynn
by Terri Page, daughter

My dad's a hero, now that's nothing new to me. He's been something of a hero to his entire family all of his life, but now it's time for a wider audience to admire him. Dad, on the other hand, would not like to be called a hero at all. So, let's call him a quiet hero, and do it quietly, and this brings me to the purpose of this paper. Now that he's nearly eighty he has let me in on one significant day in his life. Dad told me about his bronze star from WWII in a very humble and abbreviated way about twenty years ago. Now he's telling me the whole story and, incredibly, even though it happened about sixty years ago, the details are still sharp in his memory. Like he said, "I don't remember the date, but the day I'll never forget." Here's what he told me, paraphrased slightly, but as faithful as I can be:

I was stationed in the Pacific Theater, at first held in reserve when I served in New Guinea. The Japs were in pitiful condition, as MacArthur was starving them out. At Leyte we had to shoot our way onto the beach. That was kind of exhilarating.

Next, I was stationed near Manila in the Philippines. I was nineteen years old, thin, strong, and shy. This particular twenty four hours started when my captain, Jack Atwood, yelled out of his tent, "Lynn, come here! I've got to loan you out to Mosley for a couple of days." Captain Mosley needed a radio operator. I thought about asking what had happened to the previous radio operator, and then thought better of it, not quite sure I wanted to know. We had been camping in Perinaki (Paranaque), with the final destination being Manila, a coveted Japanese stronghold. Manila made sense to the Japanese, because it was full of rubble, crumbling walls and other such hiding places.

Captain Mosley was a handsome guy, I thought he looked like Clark Gable. He had a quick grin. He would grin first, then talk. He wore his .45[19] on his belt. I met Mosley that day and only knew him for six hours, but I can still see his face to this day.

I jumped in the jeep with Mosley and his driver and bounced along the typical dirt road for about five miles. Laguna de Bay[20] was the eventual target. We were to clean out the Japs located there. I was not informed much in the way of strategy or of the particulars of the destination. Small talk on the drive consisted of a couple of short questions. We turned right at Perinaki and then toward Manila. I was going to tie up with them as long as they needed me or until backup troops came. The driver and the jeep returned to base, leaving Captain Mosley and me to carry out the plan. We were about two miles east of Manila.

We were supposed to hold for the infantry. It's really crazy to proceed without them. Mosley, however, didn't hesitate to go on ahead and as long as he was alive, all decisions were made by him. We started walking and arrived at a high ridge. Mosley said, "Let's see what's on the other side of the hill." The top of the ridge was covered with six foot tall Kuna grass, which grows everywhere. When we looked over, Mosley said, "Hey, this reminds me of a movie." The First Calvary had huge Sherman tanks that looked like toys from our vantage point. Tanks worked fine in Manila, unlike Germany where their tanks were far superior to ours. Looking over the ridge, we saw six tanks; three tanks separated from the other three by about forty feet. They were going straight east, and every two hundred yards they would pivot right, line up on the airport, pivot left and line up on the airport again. They were progressing forward slowly to the east. The tanks were out there waiting

---

[19] .45 caliber semi-automatic, the standard issue sidearm for officers during World War II. In all, about 1.9 million .45s were produced during WW II by a variety of manufacturers. Officers, in general, did not carry rifles.

[20] Laguna de Bay is the largest lake in the Philippines.

to get permission to go in. After watching for awhile, we walked back downhill about two hundred yards.

Mosley had several objectives that required a radio operator. That meant me, in this case. First he told the 188th infantry to send in a squad of eight men to decide if the intersection was clean. Next he wanted to see about the status of the artillery, and finally he wanted to find out if the Japanese were dug in or if they were gone. Later I learned that these men were sent to recon[21] the area and destroy supplies the Japs had commandeered. In the process of slashing open bags of rice, they came across a Jap soldier and a Filipino woman bathing in a metal tub. The Japanese soldier foolishly reached for his gun. Both people were shot and killed.

Mosley confided that they were going to start shelling a place in Laguna de Bay. They had some P-38s, fancy planes with a double fuselage. "You could almost feel their breath when they went over."

Next a man came trotting up the hill; everybody runs there. Everything is potentially urgent. Mosley recognized him. He stood beside the captain, made small talk. Mosley asked him if he wanted to see a picture of his boy. Military etiquette dictated that I would dismiss myself while Mosley talked to another superior officer. Who could have known that this small example of protocol would be the difference between life and death?

I walked about thirty feet up the hill and sat down to give the men privacy in their discussion of home and family. I looked up and saw the guy running down the hill just about same time that I heard the first shell hit. My ears rang! I remember Mosley had said that if the Japs were on hold anywhere it would be the buildings at the end of the airstrip. I knew the artillery was really close because I couldn't hear it coming. If artillery fire is further away it makes a screaming noise between gun and ground. I started to jump up and

---

[21] reconnaissance

run, then decided to wait thirty seconds. I got up, ears ringing from the second shell. I ran over to the location where Mosley had been standing. Mosley was on his back, with one arm thrown across his chest. Shrapnel had sliced through his helmet and his head. Those helmets were a miserable excuse for protection. They were made for nothing more than looks. I looked at him and said over and over, "I'm sorry, I'm so sorry."

I was the only one on the ridge, but I didn't feel alone yet. I knew what I had to do in spite of the artillery. Even though I knew I was overstepping my rank, I grabbed the radio and called for "Ghostly," the password of the day that I had heard Mosley use several times earlier. "Incoming fire from the east end of Manila airport." Our guys started firing almost immediately. They had zeroed our guns in....155s.[22] I could hear them whistle when they started firing. I picked up all my gear and started down the hill. About a hundred yards down I saw guys coming toward me. "Where's Mosley?" I told them that he was dead. The man I was talking to was General Pierson. The general told the soldier with him to go check. The soldier returned and told the general that it was just like I had said. I could see his pain at the news of Mosley's death. General Pierson turned to me and asked, "Who called the artillery in?" I was leery to tell the general that I had done it, but I did. I was having a hard time talking to the general as he took down my name and number. General Pierson finally said, "He was my best friend." I told him I knew that lately they were having trouble getting bodies out. I knew of one guy that had been sacked for three days before they retrieved him. The general assured me that the grave patrol would not let that happen this time. Mosley's body was removed almost immediately. Finally General Pierson turned to me and said, "I would have done exactly what you did," and walked away.

One of the guys in a jeep told me where a unit was camped, about a quarter of a mile away. The guys in this

---

[22] The M114 155mm howitzer

unit wanted me to stay with their group, but I knew where I needed to go, so they turned me out. I told them I would get a ride back. I wanted to be alone. Surely, this isn't true! This guy isn't dead! As long as I wasn't hooked up I wasn't responsible to anyone. I felt so bitter, I wished that some Jap would look over the top of the trees, so I could shoot him.

A person gets to where, for some reason, you build up a certain amount of bravery. You don't think of it that way at the time, but it's true. I was always glad I called in the shells.[23]

By nightfall I had dug in with that infantry unit, went between where we were and the bay. I sent messages for those guys. Such a change in twenty four hours. That morning had started with me looking at that big grin and ended with a medal for doing my job. I never did find out what happened to the radio operator that I replaced.

The next day we fooled around at the camp, waiting for Mosley's replacement. I was going to get a ride back to my outfit but they wanted me to stay with the radio gear, and they would run me back when the replacement came.

When I got to my own camp Atwood said, "Lynn what did you do to get a medal?" "Nothing, I replied." Atwood bristled at my answer, saying he had talked with General Pierson. I realized then what he was talking about. He said he had a sheet of paper that said I had called artillery from the east end of the airport. Atwood said that shells fell, bracketing the airport. Japs had stolen three jeeps from us. They were going behind our lines, camouflaged. We didn't know how many there were, but later death reports gave the number at twenty two.

About a week later we were at a small airport on the edge of Manila. We lined up and shook hands with General

---

[23] A normal reaction to artillery would be to lay face down where there is some cover. Artillery fire rattles a person to the core. Instead, dad ran to Mosley, fired up the radio and did what he considered to be his duty. He saved lives through his bravery. Terri Page

Swing. He was the general over the whole division. I was kidded about the stature of the man who gave me my bronze star. He walked up, I saluted, he saluted, and without a word, he gave me the medal.

Second Island Luzon
Just a Minute with Three Paratroopers

By Reverend Bob LeRoy

This story was copied from the pamphlet prepared by Rev. Bob LeRoy, who was a trooper with the 511ᵗʰ Parachute Infantry Regiment. This story tells who our people were and what they did in conquering Manila.

Three Paratroopers

This true story begins at Taccoa, Georgia where the first parachute regiment of the 11ᵗʰ Airborne Division was activated in November of 1942. It was called the 511ᵗʰ Parachute Infantry Regiment, composed of three combat battalions, a service company, a medical detachment, and a headquarters company of officers and men. Over all, Headquarters Company of the Third Battalion was the group to which these three young soldiers belonged.

Sgt.[24] M. Lowe was a Baptist from South Carolina. Pfc.[25] Bob LeRoy was a Bible Presbyterian from Washington State, and Pfc. W. Judson was an independent Christian from Ohio. All three men were clean cut "Bible believing soldiers" having no use for immoral living, profanity, liquor, or tobacco.

Served God and Country

They were in the military to do a job and to do it well for God's glory and their country's victory. As Abraham Lincoln so clearly put it, "Let us have faith that right makes might and in the faith let us to the end, dare to do our duty as we understand it." The Bible, God's message to humanity, states it simply, in II Timothy Chapter 2 Verse 4: "No man that warreth entangleth himself in the affairs of this life, that he may please Him (God) who hath chosen him to be a soldier."

---

[24] Sergeant

[25] Private First Class

Tough Training Required

After taking basic training at Camp Mackall, North Carolina, special parachute training at Ft. Benning, Georgia, and heavy maneuvers at Ft. Polk, Louisiana, they finally sailed together across the big Pacific Ocean for New Guinea. Here they continued with intense jungle training for several more months, through the swamps and insect infested "bush" as they hiked and crawled over the largest island in the South Pacific campaign. In a few weeks they would be in a life or death struggle with a powerful military force that seemed fearless.

Philippine Invasion

It happened in the fall of 1944. Together they invaded the small island of Leyte in the central Philippines. Through the tangled jungles (often in hand to hand combat), they fought the catlike enemy. Their division finished the special task of clearing the mountains and the interior of all enemy resistance in record time.[26]   Then came the parachute invasion of Luzon with these same three men still kept alive by God's protective power. They marched, prayed and fought their way into the outskirts of Manila. Here took place one of the toughest and greatest battles of the Pacific War. There were no boys in this fight; only men, blood, sweat and tears.

During the U.S. attack upon Nichols Field[27] where several thousand Japanese marines were "dug in" behind large field guns and other heavy weapons, Pfc. LeRoy was shot in the left shoulder by a concealed rifleman. Sgt. Lowe (the light machine gun section sergeant) was first to his side. He quickly stopped the flow of blood from the deep wounds. The enemy's bullet had passed by this young man's heart by less than one inch. Some believe that God Almighty stood guard within that small space, guiding "the piece of death" away from LeRoy's heart, so that his physical life

---

[26] *11th Airborne Division History* page 59

[27] Held by Japanese forces since December 28, 1941

might be spared. He is still alive and now serving God as a teacher and evangelist.

Death Separates Three Soldiers

Pfc. Judson, also a devout Christian, was suddenly hit by a piece of enemy shrapnel. It happened only a few short days after LeRoy had been hit. This was a strange and sudden death, for no one else nearby was killed or even wounded by this direct hit upon Judson from an enemy gunner. It may have been that he was the bravest and best of the three soldiers, yet his life was taken. As to why LeRoy and Lowe should live, and Judson should die, only God can give the answer.

Lowe Receives Distinguished Service Cross

At this particular battle at Nichols Field, Sgt. Lowe was not wounded, but a short time later he lost one of his eyes due to a piece of flying shrapnel that destroyed the function of this vital part of his body. General Douglas MacArthur (Supreme Allied Commander) and General Joseph Swing (11th Airborne Division Commander) both recognized Sgt. M.T. Lowe as being one of the bravest and "fightingest" soldiers in the South Pacific war. They showed their appreciation to Lowe by not only promoting him to the rating of Lieutenant, but also awarding him the Silver Star[28] and Distinguished Service Cross.[29] This was the highest military medal presented to any living soldier in the entire division. One of his now historic achievements still speaks for itself.[30]

Near Bagumbayan just south of Haganoy, Lieutenant (then Tech. Sgt.) Mill T. Lowe had a light–machine gun section of twenty-four men from the 511th Parachute Infantry.

---

[28] The Silver Star, officially the Silver Star Medal, is the United States' third highest military decoration for valor that can be awarded for gallantry in action against an enemy of the United States.

[29] The Distinguished Service Cross is the second highest military decoration that can be awarded; it is given "for extreme gallantry and risk of life in actual combat with an armed enemy force."

[30] *11th Airborne Division History* page 92

His position was along the shore of Laguna de Bay, three hundred yards from any supporting troops. Repeated "banzai attacks" were made on the position by an enemy force of approximately three hundred "do or die" Nips. Sgt. Lowe personally manned a machine gun and directed fire of the others. Shooting furiously, the section drove off four attacks. Ammunition was low after the fourth attack was repulsed, so Lowe led a raiding party outside the perimeter and captured seven Jap machine guns, two mortars, and an ample supply of ammunition. Manning the captured guns, Lowe and his men broke up the fifth charge. The furious Japs then launched a sixth attack from both front and rear. Lowe constantly exposed himself to the hostile fire while coordinating the fire of the section and personally killing eight Japs in hand to hand combat. After this sixth attack was beaten off, the Japs withdrew, licking their wounds and dragging their wounded, and leaving behind a large number of dead. During the action Lowe himself killed over fifty Japs. His outstanding leadership and heroic actions were unquestionably responsible for repelling six fanatical attacks by an enemy force outnumbering his own by twelve to one. For this heroic action, Lieutenant Lowe was awarded the Distinguished Service Cross.

Patriotism Plus Religious Convictions Give Courage
     What gave these three men the courage and willingness to fight and, if necessary, die for their country? Some would say it was pure patriotism for the United Stated of America. Others might think it was the self preservation instinct, exerting itself to the fullest degree in time of war. Still others would confess that some men are born to be "fighters" while the great majority of civilized men are "peace makers" at heart. Yet not one of these three reasons is entirely correct because world history has shown us time and time again that any great military force or leading nation is what it is because of its major religion. Christianity Is Still Alive

     All during the brief history of our United States "true fundamental Christianity" has been the salt that has kept our nation reasonable, strong, and pure from within. The simple basic teaching of Christianity is this: God, who created the human race, still loves you and me. And he has provided through the Bible a clear, practical way of living a life pleasing to him (to displease God is called sin). Notice Romans 3:23 and 6:23: "But since all people have displeased God in one way or another, God had to step down from heaven and become physically born as a baby boy, with a human mother, in order to redeem the human race." This event (as fantastic as it may sound to you who are hearing about it for the first time) actually took place in history, over 1960 years ago. We set apart each December 25th as the birthday of this God man, who was and still is called the Lord Jesus Christ. His name means savior, and he came into this world to save all (past, present, and future) people from their sins.

The Important Thing

Now the most important thing in this busy life of ours is to *know* that Jesus Christ gave his life for our own personal sins. To believe in Christ, only as a general savior, is not enough. To simply believe that he was the greatest man or teacher that ever lived is still not enough to save you from your sins, but to receive him (along with the holy spirit) into your heart in a very deliberate and personal way will literally give you forgiveness of all sins, eternal life, and the peaceful assurance that God immediately has a new home prepared for you in heaven. Read 1 Peter 1:4-5.

Christ the Eternal Answer

Whether you be a serviceman or civilian, right now as you read these words, you too can receive the Lord Jesus Christ into your heart by faith, believing once and for all in him (note John 3:16). Only when you have put your complete trust in Christ and begun to live the Christian life (as these three young paratroopers did, with God's help) can you really say as Saint Paul did: "For me to live is Christ: and to die is gain."

If you are already a Christian, but would like to have a closer walk with God, first *obey* what it says to do in the

Bible. Then, secondly, spend a little time each day talking to God (prayer) alone by yourself. After this habit is formed, try memorizing a special verse once a week from your Bible reading. Before long you will be surprised to see how God is using you as a good witnessing soldier for his son, Christ Jesus our Lord. Besides all this, you will receive such an inner happiness (blessing) from serving God in this simple, sincere manner, that the world cannot help but notice that you are a joyful follower of Christ.

My honest decision

Realizing that I am a sinner, and believing that Christ, the son of God, died for my sins, I here and now receive him as my personal Savior. I yield myself absolutely to him, and by his grace I will serve him faithfully and will acknowledge him before others.

Signed _____

Date _____

Address _____

Biblical Enterprises Inc.
PO Box 48
Langley, WA 98260

The War Winds Down
Bill Rudolph, Plane #2
August 30th, 1945

The following is a first person account of riding a very early plane (perhaps the second one) into Japan on August 30th, 1945. Compiled by William Kitchen.

General Joseph Swing was the first ranking American officer to enter Japan at the surrender of that nation, and because he wanted his communications people right with him, a team of the 511th Airborne Signal Company was among the very first to enter Japan. This account was obtained from an interview at our reunion in Myrtle Beach, South Carolina, in 2001. The man interviewed was William Rudolph. What follows is his first person account of that plane entering Japan.

Bill Rudolph:
As you remember we got word that we would go into Japan when we were at Lipa in the Philippines. We rushed to Okinawa Island, and there we sat for more than two weeks until the moment finally came to move.

I was in charge of loading the plane, and in the plane was a spare tire laying down on the floor. I later learned that it was supposed to be secured up against the bulkhead. I loaded the jeep and two trailers behind the tire, lashed them down and was all ready to roll. When the plane captain came in and said, "Who loaded this plane?" I feebly confessed that I had been the one, and he said "We will never get off the ground, and there is not time to reload and re-lash, so you guys all get as far forward as you can, clear up by the cockpit."

This was a C-54 and there were six men including myself, Richard Turrentine, Al Cottone, and I cannot remember who else.

The pilot revved that plane up to max, released the brake, and it rolled along seemingly forever, and finally began to lift. We were so low that as we flew out over

Buckner Bay I could look down and count the individual coral heads on the reef.

After the plane finally reached suitable altitude, the pilot told us, "The lightest man can go back and sit in the jeep, the others will have to stay where you are up here between the fuel tanks." I was the lightest man, so I got to go back and sit in the jeep, a fact that was rubbed into me at every opportunity for the next four months we stayed in Japan.

One of the items carried on that flight was the code machine. Some called it the SIGABA machine. I was in charge of that machine and was ordered not to leave it unattended.

As we flew in over Tokyo Bay there were ships in the harbor. We were very glad to see them because we knew that they were carrying Marines. However, they were still making wakes, and I am sure that our plane landed before those ships tied up to the dock. This opinion validates the claim of the 11th Airborne of being the first American troops into Japan.

As soon as we reached Atsugi Airstrip, our first stop in Japan, we set up the message center. In just a few moments, we had established contact with MacArthur's H.Q. in Manila.

At about this time a news photographer said to me, "Go and help them raise that flag." I would not go and do that because I was responsible for the code machine. I think that I told Cottone to go and help with the flag raising, but it is too long ago to be sure. The photo came out in the Chicago Tribune next day, and my father was a faithful reader of the Tribune. I never had the nerve to tell him that I had been forced to reject the chance to be one of those who raised that flag.

Very soon one of our officers relieved me of the duty of guarding the code machine and I was told to go and carry stretchers with POWs on them. These men were too weak to walk. They had been slave laborers in Japan, and now they were going home.

Many stretchers were carried, and as I was carrying one man into the plane that we had just gotten out of, that man reached out and took my wrist . He told me, "These people have not had sugar for thirty years. If you can get sugar you will find that it is just as valuable as gold."

Our next move, made that same day, was to go into Yokohama. Our American troops were transported by Japanese trucks. The trucks were four cylinder American Chevrolets. The tires were worn out, the trucks were very dilapidated, and they burned charcoal. *Thank God* they were driven by Japanese drivers as we would not have known how to drive them.

As we were traveling into Yokohama, Japanese artillery was traveling on the same road going the opposite direction on their way to storage as part of the surrender agreement.

Along the way at about every 50 yards there stood a Japanese soldier. They were unarmed and were standing at what we called Parade Rest with their backs to the Americans. I was riding in the same truck as Captain Mabbatt, and in the back where I was seated there was a man who took great offense at the Japanese having their backs to the Americans. He stated, "The next S.O.B. that has his back to me, I'm going to blow his brains out."

As the truck approached the next sentry, that man (name unknown at this time), laid his rifle over the cab of the truck and prepared to shoot. This alerted Captain Mabbatt who wanted to know what was going on. Who knows what would have happened if Captain Mabbatt had not straightened him out by telling him the soldier was in a stance which was a posture of submission, and it was required in their culture. *Thank God* Mabbatt straightened him out and calmed him down.

The 11th Airborne Signal Company set up living in the Shell Oil Company housing that was there, which were pretty nice accommodations, especially after having lived ten months in the jungle.

Since the war was winding down, and the military was in need of decreasing its manpower, my points got me out of Japan and to Fort Lewis, Washington on Christmas Eve 1945, but the base was so full that the ship was required to go outside the three mile limit and stay there until the day after Christmas.

When I did reach Fort Lewis, the first item in the mess hall to attract my attention was a quart of milk which I proceeded to drink, only to be chastised by a German POW who was working in the cafeteria. I told him to shut up. "We won the war." I expect that I told it with too much force.

There is a sequel to the man on the stretcher telling me about the value of sugar.

New Year's Day Emerson Johnson and I had a pass, and were in Tacoma where we met a lady serving food at Thompson's Cafeteria. She noticed our 11th Airborne insignia and said, "We have had some contact with the 11th Airborne. Would you like to come to our house for New Year's dinner tonight?" Well of course we took a cab and arrived at the house. When we were seated at the table the man at the head of the table said grace. I thought the voice was familiar, but the face was not. The man said to me, "You don't recognize me do you?" Wonder of wonders, it was the man I had carried on the stretcher in Japan four months ago, the one who had told me about the sugar. Apparently the availability of food, rest, and love had worked a miracle, as the man appeared to be fully recovered.

We were guests of honor that night. I made my way home and was discharged. I married and we raised a family. Today that family is of prime importance to me. Now that I am blessed with the ability to attend reunions, it is partly for my family's sake that I want this bit of history to be recorded.

Memories of Jack Atwood

2001

From General Atwood

Signals were extremely important that day we landed in Japan. General Swing was in the first plane to land, with him as needed staff officers were Doug Quandt the G3, the Signal Officer (me), the General's aide, the G2 (Mueller) and the G4. The rest of the plane load were infantrymen to give us a little protection. As I recall the 511th Signal Company had a lot of space on plane #2 to get in radio personnel and equipment and some Message Centers.

The day we left Luzon for Okinawa I'd had to go to MacArthur's HQs in Manila for a meeting with the Chief Signal Officer on MacArthur's staff. MacArthur's Signal Officer was worried because I was the youngest Signal Officer in the whole SWPA[31] theater, but there was nothing he could do about it. It was Joe Swing's War.

The reason for the meeting was to tell the 11th Airborne to provide communications not only for itself, out on a limb in Japan, but for 8th Army HQs, and for MacArthur and staff.

I didn't get to report to General Swing on the meeting until we were settled in on Okinawa. He accepted the extra assignment with the proviso that we be allowed to use 11th Airborne Division radio call signs on all traffic rather than using 8th USA or SWPA calls.

It was a terrible day! Remember, we needed more infantry in and some artillery to protect ourselves and MacArthur. Some engineers were in after about plane #10 for road obstacle clearing, if necessary. Plus the 11th Airborne Division band to welcome MacArthur was in about plane #15 if I recall right.

---

[31] SWPA stands for the South West Pacific Area, or the Allied Supreme Command of the South West Pacific Theater of Operations.

Thanks for reminding me about this day in our lives together.

Jack Atwood, Retired General Signal Officer of the 511th Airborne *[General Atwood was 27 years old at the time.]*

The War Winds Down
Looking Back
By Henry Burgess

Note: This annotated portion is taken from the book Looking Back, *by Henry Burgess, who was a major in our outfit. What follows are some of the events that took place at the time of the Japanese surrender to officers of the 11ᵗʰ Airborne Division at Atsugi Airport in August of 1945. These are not my personal experiences, but due to the fact that they are not at all well known, I believe that they are history that needs to be known. William Kitchen*

As our lead plane entered Japan they looked down and saw the U.S. Navy in the bay. Then our planes went straight in and landed at Atsugi airport. We believe that the ships could not cross the bay and tie up at the dock in the time it took our planes to go straight in about five miles and land. Thus our claim that we were the first into Japan. We knew there were marines on those ships and we were very glad, because we were a very small outfit.

Within ten minutes of landing we had a flag up on a tin shed at the airport. General Swing — who was the first enemy officer to stand upon Japanese soil in six hundred years — had established his headquarters at the airport even though it was nothing but a table and a straight backed chair. Very soon a group of Jap officers, all of General or Admiral rank, arrived, being driven in an old Packard sedan. General Swing ordered Major Burgess "not to let them into the building" where his headquarters were. (Personally I think he wanted to humiliate them.) Major Burgess prevented them from entering the building, and then he got into that Packard and rode with them. Watching the odometer, he saw that they traveled thirteen miles to a place with "polished tables." There they held a discussion of steps to be taken when General MacArthur arrived.

At the end of this meeting, Major Burgess stood up to leave and stepped ahead of the Japanese to go out the door so they would lose "face."

"Suddenly, a general rose from the table, followed me and grabbed me by the arm. Up to that point, no Japanese had ever touched me, although several had tried." He had, after all, spent eleven months fighting them in the jungles and cities of the Philippines.

"To be honest, I was nervous and I was alone. In a natural and unthinking reaction, I knocked his hand off with my trench knife, pulled the general around in front of me with my left arm around his neck, my trench knife in my right hand with the point against his throat. Complete silence reigned."

A Jap general then informed the major that it was military courtesy for the ranking officer to leave first.

Major Burgess replied, "I am very familiar with military courtesy, and at this time one American major outranks five Jap generals."

Major Burgess did leave first. *What a man!* Thirteen miles from the nearest American.

Later as Jap officers approached General Swing, they were wearing dagger belts with daggers. General Swing ordered them, "Drop those frog stickers," to which they replied, "These are not weapons, they are symbols of authority."

Swing replied, "I understand that, and I am the authority here. *Drop them!*" – which they did.

Later General Swing wanted to inspect the troops around the airfield, and since there were no American vehicles there he took the Packard over the objection of the Japanese.

Because we went in by air, we had no American vehicles. MacArthur had ordered the Japs to have four hundred trucks there for our use. I guess there were four hundred, but they were worn out. The tires were white on the tread and they were burning charcoal for fuel. As one of our men said, "Thank God there were Jap drivers, as we could not have driven them." The 11th Airborne used them to escort General

MacArthur to his chosen headquarters at the Imperial Hotel in Yokohama.

Now I want to report an incident that took place on a truck in which Bill Rudolph was riding. I got this story from him by interviewing him at the Myrtle Beach reunion in South Carolina. Along the fifteen mile route from the airport to the hotel the Japanese had stationed either a military man or a policeman at intervals of about every fifty yards. These men stood at what we would call parade rest until the vehicles approached him. At that time he would turn his back to the vehicles. Now in the vehicle with Rudolph there was an infantry man who had been fighting them and he took great offense at their turning their back on the Americans. He said, "Next S.O.B. that turns his back on me I'm going to blow his brains out." He then proceeded to lay his M1 rifle over the cab of the truck and was prepared to carry out his threat. I thank God that action created some noise which alerted Captain Mabbatt who was riding in the front seat. He demanded to know what was going on. When he learned what it was he put a quick stop to it. He explained to the man that this action by the Japanese was an act of submission in their culture and not of defiance as he was viewing it.

We need to recognize this order to that man was one of the most important things that happened at our entry into Japan because there was a large faction in Japan who did not want to surrender. If one of those innocent guards had been so brutally slaughtered at that time, the results would have been beyond my ability to comprehend.

Just a little bit of unknown history that needs to be known.

A closing item: After the surrender document was signed aboard the USS Missouri there was great publicity over its being placed in a briefcase and handcuffed to the wrist of one of our 11th Airborne officers, a six foot plus paratrooper named Major Tom Messarau. The news cameras showed what he was supposed to deliver to the President in Washington, D.C. However there was fear that all that publicity might lead to some sort of action to interfere with its completion. So there were some Navy men dressed and acting in such a common way that you knew they were not important and were not doing anything important. These men actually delivered the document.

Japanese Officer's Question

To Paul Shea:

Here is a short story that might be of some interest.

Shortly after the signing of the peace treaty with Japan, we were given permission to travel around Japan. A day or so later I was out walking near the Shell Oil housing where the 11th Airborne Signal Company was quartered. Within only a few blocks there was what I called the Imperial Palace. This was in Yokohama, though, and I understand the Palace is in Tokyo.

At any rate this was a nice set of buildings, well painted, and the grass was well mowed, so it looked nice.

As I walked past, a Japanese officer motioned for me to come to him. I was just on the point of ignoring him when I realized it was a request, not an order. I walked over to him, and there I looked him over more closely.

Most of the Japanese were not dressed in fine clothing at all. He was in the finest uniform that I have ever seen; it was probably made of silk, or at least of very fine fabric about the color of our Navy uniforms. His chest was covered with many medals, and he was obviously of high rank.

As I walked up to him I looked into his brown eyes; he was just a little shorter than I. What was noteworthy about that meeting was what he said.

He looked right into my eyes and asked me, "Why aren't you burning and raping and looting? We would!"

What an opportunity to tell him of our God who tells us to "do good to our enemies."

I just mumbled something like, "Oh, we don't do things like that." What a wimp I was. I have regretted that for sixty years.

The man appeared genuinely perplexed. He knew how to treat fallen enemies, and he expected to receive the same kind of treatment. Had that incident been placed into the proper hands of competent officers, the progress of the occupation may have been affected.

I cannot brag about myself, but this isn't just about me, it is about the mind of the World War II Japanese.

I was close to history and didn't know it.

William C. Kitchen
January 20, 2007

My Two Bits Worth
Personal Remembrances
The Whole Thing as Lived by Me

For me WWII was more than just military experience. Experience #1 was in 1937, the Panay incident. The neighbor had come over and talked seriously with my dad; they concluded that we would be in war before the summer was over. It was a time of worry, but fourteen year olds don't worry too much.

Young William Kitchen

The next incident was while I was a senior in high school, and on becoming 18 years of age I was required to register for the draft. This I did by walking down to the post office during the noon hour. Due to the distance, and the wait at the post office, I arrived back to my next class about five minutes late. As I walked in, the teacher was annoyed and asked me where I had been. When I told her she got tears in her eyes. War had visibly reached into her classroom.

Marriage

Marge and I got married in August of 1942, and in November of that year we drove to my old home in Colorado.

On our way back to Oregon, as we were traveling in Idaho, we passed a man riding a little bay mare in the ditch alongside the road, pushing her real hard. I hadn't seen a house for several miles, so when we got a couple of hundred yards down the road it dawned on me. That man needed

85

help. I backed up and asked him if he did need help. He replied "Yes, I was supposed to report for the draft two hours ago, can you help me get to town?" He then did something very moving to me. He got off from his horse, took her bridle off and tied it on to the saddle, turned her around and slapped her on the rump so that she started toward home. He then got into our car, and we took him to the next town. It seems to me that was ten miles at least. There I let him out in front of an old store building that was obviously the local draft headquarters as there were many young men milling around and playing the universal military game of waiting.

I never saw that man again, neither did I ever forget him or my questions about him. Did the mare get home alright? Did he get in trouble for arriving late? Did he get home again? Perhaps strongest of all, what happened that day at that remote home which caused him to use that horse in such a drastic manner? He was neat, clean, and very obviously making a great effort to get to the appointed place on time. I think this man exemplifies America of 1942. If I could find him, and had the authority, I would award him a medal.

Greetings from the President

Next comes my own military experience which began with the familiar "greetings from the President."

I first reported for induction on February 19, 1943, and was given until February 26, 1943 to report for duty. On that day I left my hometown on a bus loaded to capacity. I stood next to the man who later became my brother in law, Jack Crane. In Portland we were separated according to the branch of service that we were joining. Navy Jack went one way and Army me went another.

This time we were put on a train, and during about a four hour ride I met two fellows whom I felt comfortable with. Later I learned they were both Christians, Sam Medlock and Sam Sargent. We spent about four or five days at Ft. Lewis, Washington, then Sam Sargent was sent to a tank outfit and we lost track of him.

Sam Medlock and I were placed on a train for transport to our next duty station. As we entered the passenger car most of the seats were full, so Sam and I continued down the car nearly to the end, where we found an empty private compartment. Not knowing any better we stepped in and shut the door. Nobody bothered us, and eventually the train began to move. Sam and I held that compartment all the way to Camp Mackall, North Carolina. We did not know anything about military etiquette, and neither did anybody else, so we got away with traveling in officers' quarters. After that we traveled like regular G.I.s, not like officers.

The 11th Airborne Division

When we arrived at the 11th Airborne Division, which was being newly formed, Sam was sent to the 511th Parachute Infantry and I to the 511th Airborne Signal Company.

I walked into the assigned barracks and found it about one half full of guys. Some of them were talking loudly and saying something about being from Texas. Off to one side sat a Mexican man, saying nothing. I thought, "He's going to have a tough time with those Texans." So I went over and and introduced myself; we talked for a few moments and then the army called us for something. It turned out he did not need any help with those Texans or anybody else, as he got along with everybody. My ten minuets of talk with Art Martinez resulted in three years of his care for me.

Art took very good care of me as long as we were in the army. Some times he cooked for the officers' mess, and it was not unheard of for him to call me out of the barracks at 11 p.m. saying, " I saved a couple of steaks from the officers, so come on up and eat one." You bet I helped him out when he had a problem like that.

Sam Medlock and I both learned our jobs. He learned to jump out of an airplane and fight on the ground, and I learned to gather, process and deliver the messages that kept things going. Later I was trained as a cryptographic technician and handled secret messages.

In May of 1943 my wife Marge traveled to North Carolina in the company of a friend from church whose husband, Jake, was also in the 11th. The women arrived by train in Raleigh, North Carolina, which was eighty miles from camp. I did not have money for a bus ticket to Raleigh so I hitchhiked, and Jake took a bus. I beat him there. Then, we learned there were two depots in Raleigh, so I went to one and Jake went to the other. He won, as they came to his depot.

Then came the question of lodging for the night. Jake and Vera paid $6 for their room. Marge and I looked around and found one for $3. Next day we all rode the same bus back to camp. Jake and Vera found a room somewhere, and I put my wife into a cheap rooming house, where she could

Marge and William Kitchen
First Anniversary

not sleep for the bedbugs. Army pay was not that great; I think I was getting $37 per month.

The next Sunday I got off from camp duty, and Marge and I started walking around, asking for a place to stay. We were directed to ask a certain farmer about a room, and there we ran into the incredible grace and hospitality of the south. Mr. and Mrs. Batchelor moved out of their bedroom because it had an outside door, and into another room, renting their room to us for $5 a week which included board. She was a particular lady who did things her own way. I learned to milk her cow her way, and when she knew that I was coming she always had a quart of fresh milk for me to drink. And, there were no bedbugs! Mrs. Batchelor said, "Anybody can get bedbugs, but if we get them we will get rid of them."

Maneuvers

Camp training went on and I saw my wife when I could. Then came maneuvers, in which we made a simulated attack on the U.S. My group was assigned to land in the corn field of the farm where my wife was staying. She saw us land. Now some people say that paratroopers are the dumb guys who jump out of good airplanes, and that glider troops are the dumber ones who ride in the trailer behind the airplane. I was in the latter group. It is quite a feeling to get into a glider which is tied behind a C-47 plane which is supposed to carry 24 paratroopers, knowing that the plane caries cargo and tows your glider and two more gliders. Each glider carried fourteen men plus a pilot and a copilot. Usually C-47s towed only two gliders, though sometimes three.

The air force thinks that some formula involving wings, vacuum and other factors explains what holds those things up. Little did they know that I grabbed the bench seat on either side of me and held them up out of sheer terror.

We rode out to the air field in trucks loaded just as the gliders were to be loaded. My name is Kitchen and I rode with Hoyt, Imrich, Johnson, Heltso – in other words, alphabetically. On the way out to the strip we kidded about what flowers we would send to one another.

We loaded ourselves into our assigned places, the plane warmed up, and then two radio men came running with a radio mounted on a two wheeled cart. The cart was placed right in front of me, and I was trying to find a place to put my feet when Major Atwood looked in. He said to me, "You get in *that* glider." There was no argument. I got in *that* glider, where I had to sit on the back fender of a jeep with a portion of the aircraft over my head and shoulder so that I had to lean forward and to the left. It was impossible to sit erect. We flew out over the Atlantic and returned to the shores of the United States, a trip of about two hundred fifty miles.

When we landed I heard corn stalks hitting the belly of the glider, and they sounded so loud that I thought we had overshot and were hitting the tops of pine trees which I knew were nearby. My fears were groundless, and we landed safely. But, the glider that I was first in crashed and two men were killed. Others, including Captain Hoyt were injured. My foolishness in kidding with Heltso about flowers was brought to my mind when I learned that he was one of the ones killed. I know that my position by the cart would have been a lethal one. While I had been sort of unhappy about my position in the jeep, sometimes our best interests are served, not by the convenient, but by the inconvenient.

During this particular maneuver our radio platoon performed a neat trick to solve a major problem, that of maintaining contact with Washington, D.C. This required employment of a large radio, which was normally mounted on a six by six truck. With no six by six available on an airborne operation, the radio was mounted in a glider, and

C-47 Tow Plane, repurposed as a passenger plane post war

another glider carried a jeep which was fitted with a hitch to receiver the tail of a glider.

After landing, the wings were chopped off from the radio carrying glider, causing much protest from the pilot, who declared that he had, at great effort, landed the over-loaded glider without a scratch, and now "you can't chop off the wings," to which one of our officers replied, "That man behind you, Henry Stimson, isn't worried about it." The pilot conceded the point, and I turned and saw several men in overcoats, one of whom I supposed was indeed the Secretary of War under President Franklin Delano Roosevelt.

After chopping off the wings, the tail of the glider with the radio in it was connected to the jeep, and the glider was towed backwards on its wheels.

The solution was hailed as ingenious. It would work in combat where no road connection was available. During this maneuver I was personally protected by what I believe was Divine Providence.

After that phase of our maneuvers were over, I was sent to Oklahoma to radio school. Marge took me to the train depot in a snow storm, I got onto a warm train, and she went back to her room, three thousand miles from home and alone.

We think war is a man's action, but women paid too. Civilians could travel by train but service people boarded first. This sometimes meant all the seats were filled before civilians could board. I have seen a dozen women standing by the gates at a train depot, unable to get onto a train because they were traveling alone, not escorted by a service man. I have seen service men walk up to a woman, take her by the arm, escort her to the train, then turn, going his own way, never seeing her again, knowing that his own wife might need help some time, but at least one wife was on the train. Many of these women were carrying a baby, sometimes one in their arms and one inside. Don't tell me they didn't pay. Even so we know nothing of war on our soil as the Europeans do. Fortunately my wife had no child to care for. How good God has been to our nation.

Camp Polk

I did not finish radio school, because the division was activated for overseas movement, and all personnel were ordered to report to their respective units, which for me meant going to Camp Polk, Louisiana, as that is where the division was stationed at the time.

On arrival at Camp Polk I was examined by a medical officer to determine if I was physically fit to go overseas. He decided I had a tooth that needed to be pulled, which was done. It was a bleeder, and that wasn't good as the dentist wouldn't sign my release until it stopped bleeding. I badly wanted that release so I could get a furlough before going overseas. I had to report to him the morning after it was pulled. I washed my mouth out very carefully, and told him everything was okay. He signed my release, and I got a 15 day furlough. Five days were spent going home, and five days going back, which left five precious days at home. That tooth finally quit bleeding while I was at home.

Back at Camp Polk we prepared for movement to the west coast, and all of us spent all our money so that we got on the train about broke.

Three of us, Art Martinez, Earnest Trucchio, and I played keno for five days on the way to California. Among the three of us we had a total of 27 cents, so we gambled big. Each of us lost all our money and borrowed more to get back in the game, and each of us at one time or another had all the money and loaned it to others to get back in. I don't know who was ahead when we finally broke up the game. Nobody was rich.

At Camp Stoneman, California, we did no training, but took a couple of hikes for exercise. As we hiked over the bare hills, Lloyd Marsh kept looking off to the southeast, and said home is just over there. I learned that just fifteen miles away were his wife and two week old daughter whom he had never seen. Talk about pressure. He did just what I would have done, he found a way to go home. Then cocky, ready to fight Lloyd Marsh came back talking about tiny little hands. Of course it was too good to last, and the M.P.s[32] took him away in handcuffs. That evening we had a steak dinner. So much steak was taken to the stockade and passed through the bars that Lloyd couldn't eat it all.

At Sea

We went aboard the U.S.S. Cape Clare, a former cruise ship now converted for troop transport. Lloyd Marsh was escorted aboard in handcuffs and turned over to Captain John G. Mabbatt. At once the cuffs were taken off and Marsh was back where he belonged. Nobody, not even our officers, were mad at him for what he had done. As our ship went out under the Golden Gate Bridge I stood on the deck, looking up at the traffic above us and wondered if I would ever come back, and if so when. Just then some sadist put a Jo Stafford[33] record on the loud speaker system and as that wailing voice sang "Loooong ago and farrrrrr away" I wanted to put a bullet through the speaker above my head. My eyes leaked.

I do not now know how many men were on the ship. I do know that the 188th Parachute Infantry and the 511th Airborne Signal Company were on board, and also that on the previous voyage the ship had received some damage.

It had been in the repair yard for two weeks after the rest of the division departed under convoy. We were told that we were the first troop ship to depart from San Francisco without a protective convoy. We were stacked in five bunks high; if I laid on my back in my bunk I was okay, but if I laid on my side my hips touched the man above me. I spent most of my time at the rail watching the waves and the flying fish;

---

[32] Military Police

[33] Jo Elizabeth Stafford, 1917 - 2008, was an American traditional pop singer and occasional actress.

they fascinated me. The grub wasn't bad but the conditions weren't good.

We ate in the troop mess, an L shaped room with shelves around the sides at which you stood to eat, then you moved on so someone else could eat. The weather got what I called rough, and the garbage was two inches deep on the floor. The garbage cans were semi-floating back and forth with the motion of the ship, and I just plain didn't need to eat that day.

Now, there was a crew mess and an officers mess that we could look into, and the chow looked pretty good to us. There was a rumor around that if you could get a job helping on the ship you could eat in the crew mess. My buddy Art walked in and ate with the workers. He was enjoying it until someone tapped him on the shoulder and said, "What are you doing here?" Art said "I work for the Steward." The man replied, "I am the Steward." He then said, "If you are that hungry, come back at 2:00 a.m. and I'll give you a job." Art replied, "I've got a buddy that's starving. Can I bring him too?" On a troop ship what is the difference between 2:00 a.m. and 2:00 p.m.? Thus, at 2:00 a.m. Art and I showed up and were put to scrubbing the galley, really not a bad job, all stainless steel, lots of hot water, and no pressure. The cook looked in once in awhile but as we were busy he didn't give us any trouble. We were done in less than two hours, and the rest of the trip we got to eat in the crew mess, a real boost to us. This became our routine.

The ship followed a zig zag course down near New Zealand, keeping away from expected Japanese ships. We spent twenty eight days at sea, and finally entered Milne Bay on the southeast tip of New Guinea, an impressive deep water harbor. They told us that all the navies of all the nations of the world could be sheltered in it, it was so big. There were no docks; a ship tied to the shore, and as our ship moved in under its own power, it tied to the first ship. We walked across a plank to the other ship, and across another plank to the shore. It felt good, but strange, to walk on solid ground. Ashore

We did not stay long at Milne Bay, but went on up the coast to the vicinity of Buna. I think the place was called Dobadura.[34] We went ashore by going down a cargo net carrying all our equipment into a DUCK[35] which was an amphibious truck, then to the beach to unload. Then we got onto trucks and were taken to an airstrip in the jungle. This became our home for eight months while we did some more training; more of us qualified as jumpers, and we also got accustomed to tropical heat.

Here I saw my first P-51s. A squadron of them came from the States for duty, and they gave us a show, buzzing the tents. That same afternoon as I was on duty at the message center by the side of the strip, I saw a C-47 take off. He must have tried to put on a show of his own as he only got that plane about a foot off the runway when he pulled up his wheels, but something happened, and he lost a little bit of altitude. I saw the two propellers pick up steel matting and throw it like the rooster tail of a speedboat. Of course he lost speed and wrecked the plane. I had to laugh.

I was investigated by the F.B.I. and cleared for training in the use of the SIGABA[36] system of coding and decoding messages. This meant I was in a locked room with a machine

---

[34] Doba Dura, New Guinea

[35] DUCK was not an acronym, but rather an alteration of DUKW, which was a result of General Motor's naming system of the time. D = designed in 1942, U = Utility, K = driven front wheels, and W = two powered rear axles.

[36] SIGABA was a code machine known as the most secure cryptographic machine used by any nation in WWII. "SIGABA" is not an acronym and does not stand for anything – it is simply a code word. In 1940 the Army and Navy both adopted SIGABA, and the system became operational by August 1941. By 1943, more than 10,000 SIGABA machines were in use. SIGABA machines linked with British machines to let Presidents Roosevelt and, later Truman, communicate securely with British Prime Minister Winston Churchill.

gun at the entrance and instructions to shoot *any* unauthorized person who tried to enter.

One day there was an infantry lieutenant who wanted something and was unhappy with the set up, so he started in. Jim Hemby put the muzzle of that machine gun in that officer's belly with his finger on the trigger. If that man had moved one inch the gun would have gone off. That lieutenant was extremely angry at an enlisted man who did not obey his orders, and he vowed dire consequences. We never heard any more about it, however.

New Guinea wasn't all drudgery. The Japanese had asked permission from Australia to hold military exercises on the island in the year of 1932, permission was granted, however it turned out to be an entire colony which moved in. They brought women, horses and farm equipment. Nothing was left by the time I got there but the horses. Lloyd Marsh caught a couple of them and went riding.

One thing did happen to me. Colonel Suddeth asked me to drive him to Doba Dura to the officers club. Of course I was glad to do so; getting out of camp in the evening, seeing the scenery, or perhaps something would be going on at the Red Cross center. We arrived at Doba Dura where I let him out at the officers club. He then made what he hoped I would think was a very generous gesture. He said, "You can take the jeep and go anywhere you wish to go."

One quarter of a mile down the road was an M.P. Post which I could not pass as I did not have proper dispatch papers, thirty yards away was the Red Cross center with nothing going on except some ping pong. Fifty yards the other way the road ended at the muddy beach. I went into the Red Cross hut and played some ping pong until some GI said let's go down to the beach. I could have almost thrown a rock that far but I drove there. As we sat and talked he put his hand on my knee, I thought nothing of it. Later he deliberately moved his hand up my leg. I was astonished and I turned and looked at him, my face less than a foot from his. He jumped out of that jeep and ran. I had the thought to reach under the seat, grab the jack and clobber him, but he was long gone. I had heard of homosexuals, but never dreamed I would ever meet one. So, I was dumbfounded when I did meet one and he was afraid of me.

In Carolina there occurred an incident of homosexuality, which, very properly, I knew nothing about at the time, since it did not involve me. I learned of it fifty years later in conversation with a man who was close to it but not directly involved. I'm going to include it here to show the army's reaction to it because this is an issue that has received a lot of attention lately in our changing times.

One of our officers, a colonel, was assigned a jeep and driver, another was not. The officer without a jeep requested the use of the first officer's jeep and driver. Permission was granted. The driver was instructed to drive to a remote area of the firing range.

There the officer propositioned the driver, and in return received a cussing, to which he replied, "You can't talk to me like that, I'm an officer." The driver is said to have replied, "I just did talk to you that way, because that is exactly what you are." The driver got the jeep going and left the officer out a long way from the post.

Then the driver reported to his commander, the colonel to whom the jeep was assigned. That colonel told him, "If you want anything done about this you will have to tell your story to various officers and tell it exactly the same each time. That colonel and the enlisted man went to the division chief of staff, who heard the story. They then went to the commanding general, who heard the story.

The enlisted man was dismissed, the general called for his car and driver. They drove out to the remote part of the base, and there found the before named officer. There was no publicity. The first officer, a colonel who was assigned the jeep, and who later told me the story, said that by eight o'clock that night the officer was off the base and out of the army. That is the way the army handled it at that time.

Natives

A cross cultural experience was given to me when we were permitted to attend a native festival, dance and feast. We did not in any way participate in the festival, but were assigned seating in sort of an amphitheater so that we could watch the things going on. There was rather monotonous dancing, food served on banana leaves, etc. The men wore G strings, and the women about the same. However, the women were unforgettable because of a cultural practice, which must indicate a great value being placed on a pig. Each nursing woman nursed a pig on one side and the child on the other. I saw the pig nursing, and I saw the one breast, apparently always the left one, elongated so that it hung nearly to the navel while the other one was apparently normal in size, and looked like a women's breast. Seeing things like this shows why missionaries are needed to take the gospel to people like the New Guinea natives.

One incident occurred which I think belongs here even though it did not happen to me. It does show the state of affairs that existed in a WWII Airborne unit. On a training jump, a trooper had a "streamer"[37], and he ended up on top of another man's chute. This cannot be tolerated as the weight on top of a chute will spill the air out of that chute, and both men will fall to the ground. The man on top stepped off. I do not know if I would have had the courage to do so. Either by design, by chance, or perhaps by divine intervention he stepped off so as to pass in front of, rather than behind the other trooper. As the streaming chute went by him the man with the open chute grabbed the streamer, wrapped his arms around it, and hung on. Both men rode the good chute to the ground, and both lived.

On to Leyte

When we left New Guinea, we went by ship, and the code machine that I worked on, SIGABA, was important enough to rate a state room. As one who was cleared to operate that device I was privileged to occupy that state

---

[37] A parachute that fails to open properly

room. Pretty classy for a Model-T corporal, a technician 5th grade, stripes of a corporal with a "T" (for Technician) under them, and carrying not as much authority as a corporal.

On this trip I did not have much trouble with seasickness, as I had learned on our first trip to New Guinea that once I gave up and lost my dinner, I had no more trouble on the trip. Some people didn't get over it and were sick for the entire trip. I was glad I didn't have to go through that.

Before we reached Leyte we were visited by a destroyer which passed mail aboard. I got several letters, including a package from my Aunt Dolly containing cookies and pinion nuts. The cookies were stale, but they were not going to get any more so as we ate them. The pinion nuts were not recognized by most of the guys, so I saved them until the evening.

We approached Leyte in the Philippines through beautiful indigo blue water, so smooth as to look like a mirror. A typhoon had recently passed and there was a lot of debris, including coconuts, floating around us. Some guys rigged a bucket to a rope and dipped up a couple of coconuts which they opened and ate; as I was not one of the dippers I wasn't one of the eaters.

After camp was established later that day, Art Martinez and I began to eat the nuts. They were a southwest delicacy, and Hispanic Art and I were enjoying them when we had our first air raid. In front of us a Japanese plane was shot down, and I cheered. Later I felt bad about the cheer as that was the end of a man's life.

We did not fool around as we at once set up communications; the first incident was the cutting of our phone wires as fast as the wiremen got them put up. Nobody enjoyed going out to repair the lines in the dark after they were cut, but we had no casualties from doing so.

I believe the first American landings on Leyte took place on October 20, 1944; we landed on November 18, my wife's birthday. Our landing was smooth and easy, no problems at all. A group which landed at the same place two days later suffered a lot of casualties from Japanese kamikaze planes.

Marching Inland

We did not stay around long as we were ordered to move up into the interior. Our beach was not connected to the island by any roads, as there was deep swamp all around the beach. Our engineers went to work at once to build a bridge to the mainland. The rest of the signal group and I were put onto a DUCK and went down the beach to a river where we intended to cross, but the driver went too far out into the bay where the current had slowed enough to deposit the water borne silt. There we found that the propeller would not move us as there was too much mud, and the wheels would not move us as there was too much water, so we were stuck. Now we had an air raid, and I can assure you that no one lit any matches or made any other kind of light. We did not want to be noticed at all. Later, an Alligator, which was a bigger vehicle, came out and towed us off the mud bar.

We found a road and started marching inland. At night we were shown a muddy field (all churned up by vehicles) and told to fix our camps. We ate, and I laid out my poncho as I was trained to do, made my bed in the middle of it, and climbed in and had a good night's sleep; the only problem was a colony of red ants also found my snug poncho bed-site, taking up residence in my carefully preserved and dry boots. I could not shake or dig them out, and as it was coming time to move out I was wishing for some water to rinse them out, but there was no water around. I got some gasoline from a jeep can, poured it in, and I got rid of the ants okay, but my feet paid a big price. I marched four hundred and fifty six miles that day. I know because I counted every step. I lost the skin from both my feet, but I did not lag back once, I kept up with the rest.

We set up division headquarters near the San Pablo airstrip, and while the infantry in the mountains were having a very tough time of it with the Japs and the weather, we did not have it so tough at all. In fact, being a cryptographic technician and attached to division headquarters I did not consider myself to be a combat soldier.

One day I got a memo from division H.Q.[38] in clear text stating that a Japanese pilot had been shot down. In his pocket had been found evidence that the Japanese were planning an attack on our units to commemorate the anniversary of the Pearl Harbor attack. The memo was addressed to all units, and as I was busy writing it out and addressing it to all of our units, Major Atwood[39] came up behind me, looked over my shoulder, picked up the papers that I was working on and said, "I'll take care of this." I thought nothing of the incident, assuming that he had faster ways of dealing with it than I did.

Almost fifty years later I learned that the message had originated with General MacArthur's H.Q. and had been sent to a specific officer in our unit who was trying to alert all units when General Swing, our division commander, learned of it. He, believing the Japanese did not possess the capabilities to mount such an attack, did not want all the commanders worried, so he ordered the message not to be sent.

We were well organized, and had two or more crews in the code room so that we had days off. The next day was my day off, and Captain Mabbatt asked me[40] if I could dig a ditch so as to drain off the water that was standing in front of the company headquarters. He gave me two shovels plus John Cannon, and we started digging. John took about two shovels full out and then he disappeared. Come to think of it, I don't remember ever seeing him again. I kept digging all

---

[38] Headquarters, or Head Quarters

[39] General Atwood later stated that he was not there during that time frame, therefore it had to be someone else who did this

[40] He did not order me though he certainly could have done so.

day, and got down deeper than my hips at one point. I don't know now how long the trench was, but I got water flowing out of the company area by the time retreat was sounded. I was tired but felt good as I had accomplished my objective.[41]

Being sweaty and muddy I went to a well nearby, which we had been told not to drink out of; we had tied helmets to a rope to pull up bath water. About fifteen of us were stark naked in various stages of a bath, when here came three airplanes from the direction of the fighting in the mountains.[42] We cheered, because our guys held so little real estate that efforts to supply them by air were not being successful, resulting in the Japs getting much needed supplies and our guys going hungry. They had been dropping supplies from L-5 artillery planes, and it was slow business.

Now we thought the situation had improved so that they were finally receiving real supplies. To our surprise those planes began to fire machine guns at us, and then parachutes came out of them. Those planes looked to me like our C-47s. I didn't bother to wash off the soap. I grabbed trousers as I did not want to be naked, and I grabbed shoes because if I needed to walk I wanted to be able to do so.

Wounded
About that time an equipment chute came down about fifty feet from where I was, and never having been in combat before it seemed highly important that I do something, not

---

[41] I talked with Orvile Matheney not too many years ago, and he told me that he rode the same troop ship home as John Cannon.

[42] On November 18, 1997 I learned that the Jap army unit our men were fighting in the mountains was the 26th Division, the unit that conducted the infamous Bataan Death March. On November 1, 1944 there were 20,000 of them; on December 1, 1944 there were fewer than 200. The 11th Airborne destroyed that division, the same men who ran the Death March, as the Japs did not rotate their men home as we did.

just stand there. So I fired a full clip of fifteen rounds of .30 caliber carbine ammunition into the bundle.[43]

I was not the only signalman there, but most of them were behind me. Others were firing at that thing too. Suddenly, I was feeling guilty about firing a full clip of bullets into what I knew was not a legitimate target, when a real one might come around the corner at any moment.[44] I also knew Sergeant Bob Main was behind me, as I had just seen him there.

I felt something hit me in the left shoulder and half spin me around. I thought Bob must have thrown a rock at me to tell me to quit wasting my ammunition and to save it for a more needed use later.

Looking around I saw no one, and began to move back to where the rest of the guys were. As I tried to reload I was shaking so that I had trouble reloading my carbine. Several moments later I found that my left shoe was wet, and I wondered why as I had not stepped in any water. I looked down and saw that the shoe was full of red stuff. Stupidly I stared until I realized it was blood. I'd been hit. No pain, none whatsoever after the feeling of being hit by a rock.

I then realized that somebody had fired a round into me. I knew I had been hit, but I did not know by what, as it did not hurt. My first feeling was that I was *not* a combat soldier, and I certainly did not expect to be in any fighting.

A medic was walking by, so I approached him and he put some sulfa powder on my wound, and then a triangle bandage on it. I didn't know him, and never saw him again.

---

[43] It turned out that it contained hand grenades and small arms ammunition.

[44] Virgil Adamson, an ex-infantry man and smarter than I was, slit the bundle open with his trench knife, and carried it all over to the stream and dumped it into a deep spot. He then wrapped the chute around a rock and threw it in too so that it could not be seen. I don't think that the Japs ever got that stuff.

He was just doing his job. I went across the road to some trenches and crawled in.

I spent part of that night in that foxhole, listening to the machine gun and rifle fire around me. At one point, Captain Mabbatt told me to go back across the creek and up the road to bring up some needed supplies that had been left. I started to go, and some one said, "Not him, he's been hit." Captain Mabbatt looked at me and sent Art Martinez instead.

Captain Mabbatt then told me to go to the aid station, across the road, which I did. I did not like the aid station at all as it was just the A-frame part of a roof from a small building. You could not so much as stand up in it. I was sent to the back part of the shelter and told to lay down. There was water running through the area where I was sent, so I went out and got a machete and cut some bamboo to raise me up out of the water, then I laid down, but I didn't sleep much because I could hear the medics working on seriously wounded troops all night. And, there was machine gun fire, airplanes flying overhead, and lots of other activity.

The Japanese did occupy the air strip that night. The next morning, I saw General Swing lead out a platoon, and they were part of the force that retook the strip. More troops came

---

Marge Remembers

Bill wrote a note to me every day, so I knew when I hadn't gotten a letter for two weeks that something was wrong. And, of course I was scared. When he got wounded, I got a letter in the mail from his commanding officer before I got it from the government. And he wrote such a nice letter that it made me feel a lot better. It was a relief, because at least Bill was alive! I didn't know where he was or what condition he was in, but at least I knew he was alive, which was a great relief.

I was staying with my sister Nellie and brother-in-law Chuck, and they were a great comfort. They thought as much of Bill as I did. Almost! Bill was able to write after about two weeks. I only knew he was in the hospital. I didn't know where he was. They were not allowed to say. His letters came regularly after that point, and I knew he was up and moving around.

from other directions to help in retaking the strip.

I laid around most of the day, and about dark they loaded a bunch of us onto an ambulance, and we started on the trip to the coast and to a hospital.

The Hospital

I, as one of the lesser wounded, was placed on the bench seat and told to steady the stretcher suspended from the ceiling. The ride was rough, and the man on the stretcher had a bad time of it. Finally we arrived at Tacloban[45] where the school gym was in use as a hospital. One corner of the school roof was blown off, and the hole was covered with a canvas.

This is totally irrelevant, but out in front was a beautiful 1941 Plymouth with just a few holes in it. I thought I could get it going if I had a chance. Of course that was not a real priority just then, but who says I had to be practical? I was wounded.

Inside we were lined up on canvas cots and a medical officer came by and tagged us for the order of treatment. Next to me was a colored man with a head injury, he was delirious and the officer marked him for tonight treatment, he looked at me and marked me for "in the morning treatment." Later a Major came walking by and stopped in front of me; he looked at me, called an orderly, and said, "Take him now." This was about 36 hours after I had been hit, and I had received no treatment other than the triangle bandage. I would like to know now what he detected to make him move me up like that.

Surgery

I got out of bed and started to walk to surgery, but the orderly told me that the surgeon would kill him if he let a patient walk into surgery, so I was carried into surgery, where I was given Pentothal sodium. From there all I know about the surgery is that I woke from a pleasant sleep,

---

[45] Tacloban is in the northeast portion of Leyte.

looked at the sun shining, and decided that I didn't have to get up so I turned over and went back to sleep.

When I did wake up from surgery I felt fine and was able to wander around the area. I kept hearing a big one-cylinder engine running. So I started walking toward the sound. Across the school ground, through a field, across a swamp, and up a hill. There I found the engine, powering a rock crusher. It was a diesel, had a plate on it that said it was made in the U.S. in 1898 and shipped to Manila to power a printing press. Later when the press was modernized to electricity the engine was adapted to power a rock crusher where it served until it was taken by the Japs, who used it for the same purpose until it was retaken by the U.S. GIs. Now they were using it for the same, much needed purpose. We needed a lot of crushed rock as the roads were very bad as a result of the 23 inches of rain the first thirty days we were there. I enjoyed seeing the engine, and talking to the operator; it was well worth my trip up the hill. What did the medics think of my trip? I don't know and I did not discuss it with them.

On to Saipan

Then it came time for evacuation, and I learned I was going to Saipan[46] to a hospital. Some others were being sent to New Guinea. It wasn't a matter of choice, you were sent. I got aboard the first C-54[47] I had ever seen. I was a little nervous on take off as it seemed to me the run was very long on a strip that was just low and not very much above the water in the bay. We got up okay, though. Again I was one of the more ambulatory of the group. Here I met the nurses of the transport command; I was impressed by the way they cared for the seriously wounded. Our trip was several hours long, and sometimes we looked down on ocean, and sometimes on clouds. It was beautiful and I enjoyed it.

---

[46] Saipan is the largest island of the Northern Mariana Islands in the South Pacific. It is about 1435 miles from Leyte.

[47] The Douglas C-54 Skymaster was a modified civilian Douglas DC-4, a four engine propeller driven plane.

We landed on Saipan, and were taken to the hospital. Which one? I think it was the 371st field hospital, possibly the 374th, but I'm not sure of that number. I was admitted to the hospital on December 12, 1944, after having been shot on December 6th 1944, so a lot took place in a few days. My first experience on Saipan was an air-raid. There were no fox holes, so I climbed under a D-8 cat with a bulldozer blade; it seemed to be the best option I could find.

The hospital was still in tents, several of them pitched in a row, with dirt floors. The wind blew, the dust flew. The canvas was hot, and the nurses were busy. I was operated on again and I guess they did a more thorough job than was done on Leyte. I found my medical records and read that they had used a steel brush to remove the infected tissue of my shoulder. The nurse found me reading and had a fit, but we both survived.

The wound was made by a rifle bullet entering just over the fifth vertebra, and exiting the point of my left shoulder. It seems to be almost impossible to do that without breaking bones and tearing things up in general, but I have the scars to prove it. The record states that it was a Japanese bullet that did the damage, but the Japs were in the air, and I was on the ground in the prone position for rifle firing. Thus the bullet would have exited through my chest. I have always thought that it was an American bullet fired by a trigger happy G.I. I really couldn't complain too much after the way I fired my carbine at what I knew was an equipment chute.

Work

I soon got busy. The first thing I did was carry my tray back to the nurses station after a meal, then I picked up others, then some guy asked me to bring him a urinal. The nurses were still very busy. We had no laundry and no floors. Imagine keeping things clean like that. One day the head nurse asked me if I could wash some dirty bedding. We had men injured so badly as to be unable to control their body functions, and their bedding was like a diaper. No, I did not want to wash that bedding, but I was not nearly as busy as the nurses, and certainly not trained as they were, and not as valuable. So, I told her that if she could get me hot water and soap I could do it. Well, she got them for me, and I washed the linen. Soon after this we moved into a new Quonset hut hospital that had been under construction. Very nice, with a dry roof in rain and good floors. It had hot water and mosquito nets. We all appreciated the move. Best of all they had a laundry.

By this time I had begun to accumulate a uniform; up until now I had been in a hospital gown. I kept my eyes open and found trousers here, a shirt there, and finally, a Marine died leaving a pair of size 8½ shoes. I wore a 9½, but I put the 8½s on, got them wet, and wore them while they dried. It worked. I could now shed my useless sandals.

I also got a job. I was given the job of passing out vitamin pills and juice to each man at mid-morning, and also running errands. Many Iwo Jima and Okinawa causalities were coming in and they thought that I was hospital personnel. I got other privileges, too; I could go to the PX[48] and to the staff movies at night. I even got to go out on the road and hitchhike around the island, several times.

I had been carrying my left arm in a sling; some time later I visited the doctor. He said, "Your arm is now ready to be used." As I left his office I used my right hand to open the door. He shouted at me, "I said use it!" So I backed up and opened the door with my left hand.

The doctor then gave me swimming privileges in what must be the finest beach in all the world, a crescent three miles long, a quarter of a mile out to the reef. You could wade almost all the way to the reef, and if you found yourself unable to wade you could take a dozen swimming strokes and wade again. You had just passed a bomb or shell hole. Water temperature was just perfect; you could stay out all afternoon.

---

[48] PX is short for Post Exchange, a place where a soldier could purchase goods not provided as part of the basic equipment.

There was a section of beach off limits to us as it was reserved for the native population of the island. Mostly women and children would swim in that area.

As you can see I did not suffer much on Saipan.

All in all I stayed in that hospital six months. I later learned that there was a rule that any wound which could not be healed in six months was supposed to rate a transfer to a more sophisticated hospital either in Hawaii or in the U.S. Obviously I did not rate that kind of treatment. So on the day that I had been in that hospital six months the commanding officer called me into his office and asked me if I would like to transfer from Signal Corp to hospital duty. I said "No, sir, I want to go back to the 11th Airborne." That conversation ended my hospital time. I really could have gone back sooner but I knew I was having it easy so I didn't complain.

Back to Leyte

I had come to the hospital from Leyte so I was sent back to Leyte, without regard to the fact that the 11th Airborne was now on the island of Luzon. I was sent to a replacement depot, and this sort of worried me as I feared that I might be sent as a replacement to some outfit that had suffered major causalities. Then, I met Captain Hoyt, who had recovered from his glider accident injuries, and he told me that he was unable to get back in to the 11th Airborne Division. This worried me some more as I thought if an officer can't get back, what are my chances?

I walked out of the replacement depot, dumb as it may sound. I didn't have permission. I could not bear the thought of turning down the hospital only to end up in some infantry outfit, so I went down to the beach where I found a pile of mostly junk equipment and a detail of one 11th Airborne officer and a few enlisted men to guard it. I joined them with no status whatever, but I could eat. Every few days I would hitchhike up to the airfield and ask about a plane going to Luzon. Always, it was no luck, and I would go back to the equipment, go swimming, then sleep under a palm tree.

Finally, after a couple of weeks I found a plane that could take me. I hurried, got my equipment, and returned to the airstrip in time to catch the plane.

"Home"

After a short flight, they let me off on Clark Field[49], and when I got out on the street I found an 11th Airborne. Division jeep, which gave me a ride about sixty miles down to Lipa. There I found a jeep going to Mataasnakahoy[50],

---

In my absence...

In February, while I was away, the 511th and the 188th performed an action that has been hailed as a classic military rescue.

The 188th made a diversionary attack, and the 511th parachuted onto a prison camp. The Japanese guards had been killing prisoners rather than surrendering them.

Filipino guerillas had been bringing information to American forces about the prison at Los Banos Agricultural School, which was being used as a prison housing only civilian prisoners: nuns, priests, missionaries, Standard Oil Company employees, and one Sears employee. Any person with Caucasian features found in the Philippines was there: men, women, and children. One captive was Carol Terry, later Carol Talbot[1], wife of Dr. Louis Talbot of Talbot Theological School.

The 511th, in their action, transported two thousand, one hundred, forty seven weak, ill, and starving prisoners from thirty five miles behind enemy lines to safety behind American lines without the loss of one American life. It should not be surprising that some of the prisoners remarked "they look like angels" as the troopers were parachuting down to them. We accepted the nickname and have been known as "The Angels" ever since.

The 188th, while not participating in the rescue, diverted the attention of a 10,000 man Japanese force occupying ground just eight miles from the prison, and kept them away until the rescue was completed. This force was part of the enemy that our 11th Division had bypassed on their way to Manila.

General Colin Powell has since instructed all military schools to teach the maneuver used by the 511th and 188th.

---

[49] Clark Air Base was an American military facility from 1903 to 1991. It is now Clark International Airport.

[50] According to Wikipedia, although the town's name is written as one word, it comes from the Tagalog phrase *mataas na kahoy*, which means "tall tree."

where I found the signal company and reported to Captain Mabbatt. Finally I was home.

When I saw Art Martinez he gave me a package containing my personal effects, my letters, my watch, and whatever else there was there. How do you pay for, how do you even appreciate the friendship of a man who will do such a thing for you? Through six months of fighting in hell? During my absence the outfit had endured extreme combat, first in the mountains of Leyte, then making the initial assault on the island of Luzon, landing at Nasugbu.

They had pushed the Japs out of the area[51], then dashed to Manila in what was described as a beachhead one fourth mile wide and sixty nine miles deep. Seven thousand Philippine guerillas helping us had a big part in the success of that operation. They pushed through the Japs making so much noise that the Japs thought they must be a much larger force. They entered Manila ahead of the First Cavalry by about four hours, where they met strong Japanese resistance. They were ordered to pull back across the river at Paranaque until the next morning. Meanwhile, the First Cavalry with tanks got into Manila from the north about midnight and were able to stay. Officially they beat us by six hours. They had tanks and we had mortars, machine guns and men of the highest quality. (You bet I am prejudiced.)

I returned to the outfit just as we were regrouping for the expected assault on Japan. We knew it would be tough, but we were ready to go as we knew there was no other way we could go home, and that is what we all wanted more than anything else in the world.

I returned to duty in the code room, and one morning I received, and started to decode, a message when I found a secondary code that alerted me it must be decoded by an

---

[51] Orvile Matheney later told me that as the wire platoon was unloading, the Jeeps were in deep water so they would not run. They worked on them a bit, but as the Japs were shooting at them from the bluffs above they soon left the Jeeps and went ashore without them.

officer. I left it in the machine. and the first officer I found was Captain Mabbatt. He finished decoding the message; later that day it was announced that the atom bomb had been dropped on Hiroshima.

A few days later I was again on duty when I received another message of the same type. This time the officer I found was Major Atwood, and he finished decoding the message. This time, when they were ready to do so, our division officers announced that Japan had asked for peace, and that we would be the first to enter Japan. By 10:00 o'clock that night we were airborne and on our way to Okinawa. We rode in C-54 planes, which were much larger than the C-47s we were used to.

Okinawa

Once on Okinawa, we sat for seventeen days while there were additional negotiations between Japan and the U.S. One evening we watched a white painted Jap Betty Bomber go over; we were expecting it, as it carried Tojo[52] on his way to talk to General Douglas MacArthur in Manila. Every searchlight battery on the island must have picked up that plane, and they stayed with it until it was out of range. I would think that must have been a nerve wracking experience, as it was well known that if two lights focused on a plane the artillery was also focused

---

Atomic Bomb

People today bemoan the use of the atomic bomb, which did kill about 130,000 people, a terrible price. But, consider that our G2[19] working at Japan's military headquarters found documents prepared by the Japanese War Department, assessing the cost of an American attack on Japan and being fought to the conclusion. These Japanese military experts estimated that such an attack would cost the lives of 1,000,000 Americans, and to bring about this cost they expected to lose 5,000,000 Japanese. Interestingly, this five to one ratio was just what our experience was in Leyte and Luzon. Personally, I am very glad for the use of the A-Bomb as it convinced the Japanese to concede defeat without fighting on to the bitter end, saving lives for both them and for us. My chances of coming out alive were not good as airborne troops go in far from the beaches (if they go airborne) and they go lightly equipped.   *W.C.K.*

---

[52] Prime Minister Hideki Tojo of Japan

on that plane, and a hit was almost certain. Fortunately, no one fired.

Okinawa was first hot, then wet. We had only pup tents, so some of us, myself included, went into the tombs[53], moved the bones aside and sat down. It was cool in the heat, and dry in the rain. Disrespectful? Perhaps. It was not done for that purpose, but we considered it in the light of the living needing it more than the long dead. No bones were destroyed, so they could have been replaced later.

After the seventeen long days, our unit finally got word to proceed to Japan proper, and again the C-54s appeared. We were told that every serviceable C-54 in the world with the exception of Air Force One, the U.S. President's plane, was used in that movement.

As our plane flew over the Japanese coast we could see the coastal defense works. I was very glad they were not in use against us. As we went into the city I saw the spider holes in the back yards, and I knew that entire families would be in them and our guys would have to dig them out, slowly, horribly, and at great cost to our people.

Our signal people went into mainland Japan on the second plane, as a general always wants his communications with him. Then the 511th parachute infantry provided the honor guard for General MacArthur as he arrived and took up residence at his hotel.

Japan Formally Surrenders

When the surrender was signed aboard the U.S.S. Missouri, one of our officers was standing on the deck. He is visible in the pictures only as a head behind others. He is only identified by an arrow drawn to identify him. Later, he, Major Thomas Messeau is the person to whose wrist the signed document was handcuffed for transport to Washington D.C. An unromantic note must be inserted here

---

[53] The tombs are commonly called "turtleback tombs" because of their resemblance to a turtle's shell. In some cases the tombs hold one person's remains, in others the remains from families.

as the papers he actually carried were dummy papers, for fear that a coup may be tried. The actual surrender document is said to have been carried by four drunken sailor types, men who were not drunk at all but disguised to look like persons of no importance, carrying out a very important job.

Until the signing we were restricted to quarters, but after it we had quite a lot of freedom to move about Japan. On about the second or third day after the signing I was walking on the street of Yokohama when a Japanese officer motioned for me to stop. I nearly went on because I did not obey Jap officers, then I saw he was asking me, not ordering me, so I stopped. He was a military man with a lot of gold braid on his uniform, obviously of high rank. He spoke perfect English, and he asked me, "Why aren't you raping, burning, and looting? We would." I was dumb-founded. What a chance to tell him of our Judeo-Christian ethic. Instead I just said, "We don't do things like that." Again I blew it, as at many other times in my life. I went on, and of course never saw him again.

Sendai

About this time our unit moved by truck and jeep convoy to the city of Sendai. I found the country beautiful with many tiny farms and some not so tiny. Sometimes we could see a small thatched roof house with an electric line going in, and sometimes we could see inside and see one bare bulb in the middle of the house. We went through some badly bombed villages and in one of them I saw the only act of resistance that I ever saw in Japan. One man stood on top of a heap of rubble and shook his fist at us as we passed by. Who knows what was in his mind? Near Sendai we were quartered in a powder factory, and there were some chemicals in some of the buildings. Each building had a cement wall around it for the purpose of deflecting a blast upward away from other buildings if an explosion did take place. The area was Matsushima – Pine Island, a seaside resort area once used by the wealthy Japanese. They are little islands, some connected by little bridges, many with well tended gardens, and there was even a motor launch powered by a Model-A Ford engine. Our signal guys got it going, but had to give it up.

Near our quarters were ridges with tunnels through them with steel doors on both ends. They could be opened on either side of the ridge. There must have been half a dozen tunnels, and they were all connected by a lateral tunnel running lengthways in the center of the ridge.

Inside there was a munitions factory with lathes, milling machines, and even their own power plant. Coal fired the boiler, which was so far down in the mountain that the smokestack only stuck up about eighteen inches above ground. I saw our military people carry these machines out and dump them in a swamp. Later America resupplied the Japanese nation with equipment to jump-start their post war industrial capacity; such a waste.

For roads, at rivers they had good concrete bridges and paved approaches, then gravel to the next bad spot, and again good road over the obstruction. Some of our guys complained about the way the Japs did things. Personally I thought they used good judgment fixing the worst places, with the ability to finish the job as funds were available.

Exploring Japan

I was assigned to drive a jeep picking up mail and transporting couriers as our division was spread over a large area of Japan. Officers were constantly traveling from outlying units to division headquarters and back again to their respective units. Usually they traveled by Japan's train system. One time a courier missed his train and I was able to outrun it and catch it at a stop about thirty miles north. I caught the train in the little town, and the courier got on it to continue his trip to his unit's destination. While there I got into conversation with a Japanese woman who spoke good English, but she was dressed like the peasant women around her. She told me that she had been born in the United States and was taken to Japan by her parents and left there as a young girl. She did not like being in Japan. I didn't know what I could do for her so I went back to Sendai. In about 1934, our Japanese neighbors in Colorado took a twelve year old girl to Japan and didn't bring her back with them. I think they sell them. That was my only trip up that direction, interesting.

With the irregular hours of my job I was given my own dispatch book, so I wrote my own dispatches and I could go by the MP check points with no trouble. When I did not have a train to meet I used the Jeep and especially the Dodge weapons carrier to my own advantage, taking buddies with me when I could.

We went to a Buddhist shrine near the river and I drove up the steps so we could look around. From up there on the shrine we could see a suspension bridge over the river. It was narrow but it looked strong enough to me, so I drove over it, about thirty feet above the water, and when I was over the guys got back in. Next we encountered a tunnel. It was so low I had to take the windshield off to go through. There was not room to turn around and I did not want to have to back across the bridge, so we went ahead.

Next was a ridge so narrow that the differential drug with one tire on each side of the ridge. Again I had the truck to myself, but now we found a farm and stopped to watch the men threshing grain by hand, pounding the grain, then tossing it up in the air from a blanket to let the wind blow away the chaff. The women saw us and away they went up onto the mountain. We could not speak to them and we did not want to bother them so we just ignored them, and after watching the threshers for awhile we gave them some cigarettes and went on. Next we saw a tall pine tree with a big black crow sitting in the top of it. I said to Jim Hemby, "You can't knock him down with your carbine." He said "He's a dead bird." He took one quick shot and nothing happened, so we began to jeer Jim. About that time the crow just toppled off from the limb and by reflex spread his wings so that he glided down to the ground and never moved. He was instantly dead and sat there until he fell off. The

Japanese came and got him and took him away, to eat I suppose. We didn't need him. We didn't jeer Jim anymore. We kept on going and found another way back to the camp.

The Point System

The war was over and everybody wanted to go home, so the army devised a point system, based on length of service, time in combat zone, wounds, and I don't know what else. So the older guys started going home. I had fifty three points, and finally that became enough to be my ticket home. I took out the truck one last time, and we went back to the crow tree, but not by way of the bridge and tunnel.

On the way home Bob Curtis wanted to drive. This guy celebrated his seventeenth birthday in Japan and he had been with us for three years. No wonder we had noticed that he was small. I let him drive, and he entered the HQ area too fast so the M.P. pulled us over. Bob did not have a driver's license so I passed him mine, but then he couldn't recite the serial number, so I whispered mine to him, and the M.P. wrote it down.

Now I expected to leave in about an hour and I hoped the MPs would be slow with their paperwork. As I walked out to the truck to leave I was carrying my duffel bag, and Jim Hemby[54] came up to me, knocked my hand off of the bag and said, "I'm carrying this bag." I got up on the truck and he handed up my bag. I never saw him again. The address that I had for him was not a good one.

You know, life isn't really fair. I had the wound, so that gave me a purple heart which gave me five extra points, which were enough to get me out of Japan about two weeks before all the buddies that I had served with for three years except for my easy time on Saipan and their rough time on Letye and Luzon.

---

[54] After the 1997 convention at Omaha, Nebraska, I took the time to go to Oklahoma and look up the Hemby family. I found Jim's sister, and she showed me his gravestone. If I had been one year sooner, I could have seen him in person.

I went down to a Japanese military academy named Zama near Yokohama. There I was processed for return home as soon as shipping was available. It didn't take very long, only a few days. However I was to have one more experience before going home.

One night I drew guard duty, and was assigned to guard the stockade gate. About 2:00 a.m. a man walked up to me with a sack over his shoulder and demanded to be let into the stockade. He said a buddy had let him out on an earlier shift and he had to get in before he was missed. Well how could he be lying? If he was trying to get out I would have known it was a con, but in, it must be true. So I opened the gate and he went in. They had a fire going and were soon roasting vegetables over the coals. I said nothing and finished my shift. I never heard anything more about it, so I figured why stir up a can of worms by asking?

Homeward Bound

Finally, the ship was ready to load. I got on, and we left Japan. We were seventeen days crossing the North Pacific in December, 1945. The weather seemed to be quite rough to me, but we were going home so nothing could bother me. On the seventeenth day we sailed into the Straight of Juan de Fuca, down Hoods Canal, and into the port of Tacoma.[55]

Sailing in I was very disgusted with the ship's crew as they threw overboard all the mattresses that the officers had been sleeping on. Then they threw overboard whole sides of beef. I supposed they wanted to get all fresh provisions for the next trip out, but I didn't like what they did with the old supplies.

I got into Ft. Lewis, Washington not nearly as afraid of the military as I had been last time I saw that place. We were

---

[55] During the war both my father and my wife worked at the shipyard in Portland. I later learned that the ship I came home on, the U.S.S. Drew, was built in Portland, and that my wife had worked on it. She spent time burning out a bad weld and then re-welding it.

served a good steak meal and all the fresh milk we could drink. I took a whole quart to start with, and had more later.

Then, I got a one day pass. I called my wife, Marge, and she came up on a bus and met me at Longview, Washington. We stayed at the same hotel where we had spent our wedding night, a real flea bag of a hotel, but at the time I didn't know any better.

Next day she went back home, and I went back to Ft. Lewis. Soon my processing out was finished and I could go home. As I went out the last door there was a sign, "Enter here if you think you have a claim against the government. "I went in and showed them my wound. At the time I came home the scar on my back was just as deep as two of my fingers were wide. My record stated that one muscle had been removed. I wondered how much trouble this would give me in later years and as I grew older. I was awarded 10% disability. I have not experienced difficulty with my arm but at that time I just didn't know.

Portland

I got on to a bus and got into Portland to the bus depot at about 12:30 a.m. There was a bus scheduled for departure in the morning at 7:00 a.m. I was only fourteen miles from home, and I was in no mood to sit and wait for a bus. I threw my bag over my shoulder and started walking east. I was walking along the bus route, and figured that even if I walked all night and had to catch the bus on its way I would not lose anything, and walking was better than waiting. Besides, I knew I could walk fourteen miles in less than seven hours. About two a.m., I was crossing the Burnside Bridge, light snow falling, almost no cars on the road, and I heard someone call my name. A car stopped, and inside I recognized a girl I had graduated from high school with. She[56] and her husband were on their way home from college for Christmas. They took me to my wife's sister's house, as that is where I expected to find my wife. However she had

---

[56] Ellinore Reid Hermansen

spent the night with *my* folks, so my brother-in-law took me there. We woke everybody up and had breakfast. I changed my clothes into civilian clothes, and I was out of the Army on December 23, 1945. What a Christmas present!

I've been home for fifty years now. God has been good to us; we have good health, a nice home, a good family, all who know the Lord, and I am grateful.

This is probably far too long for your purposes, but I will print up some copies for my family. You may do as you please with this copy including destroy it. I think my family will be glad to have this narrative.

Respectfully,
W.C. Kitchen, 511ᵗʰ Airborne Signal Company

A Further Memory
I was born in 1923. My grandmother Hard died in 1931, so you see I did not know her very long. However, one time before she became ill and bedfast I was at her house and helped her do something. I have no idea what it was, but we worked at something, and as evening came and it was twilight she said to me, "Let's just sit and rest, be quiet, sit still and enjoy the twilight."

We sat perfectly still for a while, not eating, not drinking, not talking, but in very real fellowship and camaraderie. After that experience I learned to enjoy quiet rest in the evening. That is my only real good clear memory of my grandmother Hard.

In my youth we were taught a fable that I now know to be untrue, which was the idea that in old age we would have nothing to do, just sit and wait for time to pass. Not so. I am almost seventy five now and still busy, but with things that I want to do and with not enough time to do them all. Just now it is 5:00 a.m., and I am at this computer, needing to study for a Bible class, going out today to help Bill set up a big pole in his yard, wanting to have lunch with Airborne buddies if I can get there. I'm wanting to plant a garden, and

I have a fence to fix, and an animal that I want to work with but can't find the time.

I wouldn't have it any other way. I thank my God for the interest to do things and the ability to do them.

The Cost of Birthing a Soldier ~ a Further Memory

My mother, Katherine Kitchen, and paternal grandmother, Margaret Strayer, had a tradition which they continued throughout my time in the service. Every night they sang the lovely song "God Will Take Care of You." It was their prayer and solace. Their love and devotion were a great help to a lonely soldier thousands of miles from home.

The day I was wounded my maternal uncle, George Hard, experienced a heaviness of soul that would not ease. He knew nothing of my whereabouts or circumstances but felt compelled to pray for me. He prayed long and often for my safety and well being. I believe his prayers were influential in the good care I received.

War is hard on everyone!

The WWII Internment of Japanese Citizens

I have some thoughts about the internment of Japanese citizens on the United States West Coast during WWII.

The following two experiences took place in my life before WWII. By way of background, I was born in 1923, and my grandmother died in 1931. Some time before grandma died my mother moved our family into her mother's home so that she could care for her mother during her final illness.

The first incident occurred before we moved into grandma's house; it occurred during a spell of warm weather, and was certainly no later than 1930, at which time I was 7 years old.

Japanese children went to school with the rest of us for five days a week, but on Saturday and Sunday they used the local school building for Japanese instruction.

One day my mother sent me to deliver a note to a neighbor, and I had the misfortune to pass their school house at recess time, and five little boys came out into the street and pushed me around until they knocked me down. As I was laying on the ground, one of the boys said to me, "There's going to be war, and we going to fight for Japan, we not going to fight for the U.S." This is the exact speech construction that he used.

This had to have been in 1930, and the war really started in earnest in 1942, so those boys had 12 years to grow up and wise up by the time war did actually take place. I wish I had contact with some of them to learn what they really did.

The second happened while we were living in grandma's house, 1931 or 1932. I have no diary to consult so these are the closest dates that I can provide.

My grandmother was a widow, and she had rented her farm to a Japanese fellow. He planted twenty acres of cauliflower in the field nearest to the house, where he had a Japanese woman working for him hoeing that field. One day while my mother was out in the yard at her mother's house, that Japanese woman came to the house for a refill on her water jug. My mother invited her to sit and rest in the shade in the yard, which the lady did. As she rested there she talked to my mother and told her, "Pretty soon Japanese woman live in big house and white woman work in field."

Now I know that the little boys did not come up with their statement on their own. There was an agitator in that school, and I believe that the older woman got her opinion from the same source. By coincidence that school building burned to the ground the same weekend as Pearl Harbor was bombed.

These are my own personal experiences, not some hearsay. By themselves they do not justify the internment of the Japanese.

A legitimate question is, "How widespread was this feeling among the Japanese?" Another question, was that agitator a local person, or was he an agent from Japan who perhaps visited other schools as a recruiter for the Japanese army?

I personally place enough faith in our own government to believe that there was justifiable mistrust for this one segment of the population to account for the internment. Yes! There were innocent people interred. Of course no one liked to be there. Could the traitors have been identified, and separated out? I simply do not know.

I have answered no ones objections. Certainly I have not given adequate justification for this controversial action. That being said, perhaps this sheds just a little bit of light on the subject.

Respectfully,
William C. Kitchen
511ᵗʰ Airborne Signal Company

Marge Kitchen

While sitting in a hospital waiting area, Mr. W. C. Kitchen saw an advertisement in Farm & Ranch Living *magazine. Doubting that his wife Marge would respond, he instead wrote to Lisa Smelser, who had placed the advertisement. Ms. Smelser, a high school sophomore, was looking for "real-life Rosies" from WWII for a school project, and struck gold in Marge Kitchen. The following is taken from Ms. Smelser's 2003 book,* Real-Life Rosies: The Women of WWII, *and is told from Mr. William Kitchen's perspective.*

My wife Marge graduated from high school in Chester, Nebraska in June of 1940. She moved to Oregon that fall, and married me on August 16, 1942. I went into the service on February 19, 1943. I was sent to [North] Carolina for training, and she came to me when she could and stayed as long as she could.

Then on May 15, 1944, I went over to New Guinea and on up to Leyte, Saipan, Luzon, Okinawa, and mainland Japan. We raised the first American flag over Japan on August 30, 1945. But this is supposed to be about her. When I left, she went to welding school and went to work in the shipyards here in Portland, Oregon.

In one thirty day period they launched twenty three ships, one every thirty hours. I am impressed and hope you are too. For a time she worked ten hours per day, seven days a week.

One incident which I doubt if she would tell you about is the time she went on strike. She, as a welder, was assigned to a crew which contained, among others, some ship-fitters. Now, as the name suggests, that classification was to make the flat steel plates fit the exact contour of the ship. On this particular day they showed her a plate that did not match up by about two inches and told her to weld it up. She refused, and that sub-foreman fired her. She refused to leave because she knew they would get someone else to weld it and it would not be a safe job. They went and got someone else who did have enough authority to fire her, and when he saw the job she refused to do, he told those ship-fitters to redo their job, which they reluctantly did. They were just lazy and wanted her to cover for their shoddy work, which she refused to do. She told them her husband might come home on this ship.

Later her crew was sometimes the finish crew, the last crew to leave the ship. They had to redo any work that was rejected by the inspectors. On one ship she spent a lot of time burning out a bad weld on the rudder attachment and then re-welding it. That is the ship I came home on.

I got on that ship in Yokohama on December 5, 1945, and had a stormy North Pacific crossing and arrived in Washington State on December 22, and was home on December 24, 1945. What a homecoming. What a Christmas.

Mrs. Kitchen Tells about Her Time As "Rosie":

...I spent my childhood and teens in Nebraska at the little town of Chester, the first town in Nebraska across the Kansas-Nebraska border on Highway 81. My parents moved to Oregon to be near my sister in 1940. I fell in love with this country and never wanted to go back to Nebraska, but of course we went back for a visit and found a lot of beauty there also...

Young Marge

I worked at the Oregon Shipyards in Portland, Oregon. I started to work in 1944 and my work was completed at the end of the war. Our main purpose was to build ships and build ships we did. One a day for awhile. I worked as a welder on what they call the "ways." This is where they started and finished the ship ready to launch it. I was on one of the crews that was the last to leave the ship before it was launched and went to the docks to be finished. I did spend a little time there, but only as a backup when they were behind.

The dock was completely different than on the ways. It was finish work and the ways was all rough work putting the ship together.

When I started to work I went to welding school and got paid to learn they were so short on help. I had to learn from the start. How to strike an arc and how to weld flat, overhead, and vertical. We had to pass a test before we could go to the yards. As welding schools are today we didn't learn very much. We only had a few kinds of metals to weld on, so we didn't learn anything about metals or how to weld on different kinds. Today they have to learn all of those things. We were at war and in an emergency and didn't have time to learn all of those things.

Our ships were called Victory ships.

I believe they were mostly used to transport troops to the battle zone. My husband came home on one of those ships.

I had different reasons for working. One – I needed a job pretty bad as my allotment was only $50.00 per month. Then, my country needed help.

There were a lot of women working at the yards. On my crew there were four women and two men. One man was too old to go to war and the other one had been turned down. I have no idea how many people worked there – a lot. There were three shifts and for many weeks we worked seven days a week. My hourly wage was $1.25, which was pretty good wages for that time. I guess the best part of working there was that I made new friends, and the worst was the cold and the heat. The metal wasn't very forgiving when it came to temperature. I would find a board to stand on so my feet wouldn't get so hot and so cold.

Yes, I liked my boss. He gave us a job and expected us to do it right, and most of the time he left us to our work. I liked my coworkers, they were good workers and we had no bickering, we just did our jobs and helped the others if needed.

When I was going out to the yards I had heard a lot of bad stories about how the guys would treat me, but I never had any problem at all. I think most of the stories were told to scare you.

I felt good about my contribution to the war and I don't know that it helped me any, but it certainly didn't hurt me.

Victory Ships

The **Victory ship** was a cargo ship produced in large numbers by North American shipyards during World War II to replace losses caused by German submarines. Based on the earlier Liberty ship, but with more powerful engines, 531 Victory ships were built. Victory ships were slightly larger than Liberty ships, at 455 feet long and 62 feet wide with 28 feet draft (loaded). They had a different appearance from Liberty ships. To make them less vulnerable to U-boat attacks, Victory ships made 15 to 17 knots, 4 to 6 knots faster than the Libertys, and had longer range. The extra speed was achieved through improved engines. The Atlantic battle had been won by the time the first ships appeared; only two were sunk by U-boats, the *Fort Bellingham* and *Fort St. Nicholas*. Three more were sunk by Japanese Kamikaze attacks in April 1945, *Logan Victory*, *Hobbs Victory* and *Canada Victory*.

From *Wikipedia, the free encyclopedia*

Red Oak Victory, now a museum ship

Mr. Kitchen Tells of a Later Incident Involving His Wife's Welding Skills

One incident is so memorable that I must tell you about it as she will not. The old car that we drove at that time was a Model-A Ford. Its brake system was not like the modern cars, but consisted of levers and steel rods to each wheel. One day, as we were driving, one of those steel rods broke. It was dragging on the ground, plus we only had three brakes. I stopped at a nearby shop and asked the operator if he could weld my brake rod. He said he could, and he prepared to do so. He clamped a piece of metal to the broken rod, put the rod in place, and clamped it there. Then he took his welder and went under, but there was never the sound of a welder in action. At last he came out looking discouraged, and Marge said, "May I try?" He said okay, and she laid on his creeper and scooted under; at once there was the sound of a welder going. In about one or two moments she came out and got into the car. I asked the man, "What do I owe you?" He said, "Nothing, Mister," and we went on down the road. I have remembered that for a long time...with a smile.

Not All Battles Are Fought on the War Front

Not all of the battles of the war were fought on the foreign battle field. For instance, my sister broke the law as she was leaving the employ of the shipyard. There was a wartime law that anyone working on a critical wartime job was "frozen to the job" and anyone who quit such a job was subject to penalties and punishment. My younger sister, Lorraine, was working the 4:00 p.m. to midnight shift as a production welder at the Oregon shipyard in St. Johns, Oregon. One night at quitting time she put her time card into the machine to have it stamped according to standard procedure. But instead of putting it back into the assigned slot she handed it to the guard who was standing there and told him she was quitting. He informed her that according to the law she could not quit. He asked her why she wanted to quit and she told him,

"Because school starts *TOMORROW*. I'm seventeen years old, and I'm going to *FINISH* high school."

I'm proud of her! Could you arrest her?

Lorraine was not the only family member to work in the shipyard. My father, Harold Kitchen, worked there as well and through his help, my wife Marge joined the workers in the yard as a welder. Lorraine passed her working gear on to Marge. There were leathers (a type of overall), gloves, and helmet. Marge had some experiences there that were very important. She learned welding at the yard. One hard lesson was to slow down when making multiple pass

Lorraine's, and later Marge's, welding gloves

welds. She had to learn to allow the metal to cool before going over it again and generating more heat. The heat would change the structure of the metal so that when put under stress it would break. Thanks to a creative teacher she mastered this technique and it may have been instrumental in saving lives.

In the early days of her job her crew was assigned to weld in the double bottoms, a cramped and smoky place between the inner and the outer bottom of the ship. She found this so claustrophobic that she just did not think she could continue to work there. Her supervisor encouraged her to be patient because he knew their crew would soon be moving to other locations. He was very considerate of his crew and saw to it that the air quality was kept good and that their supplies were well at hand. That got her through a very difficult time.

A short time later her crew was indeed assigned to work on another part of the ship. On one particular day she was assigned to work as the welder with some shipfitters[57] working on the hull. Unfortunately there was some sloppy work going on. At one point they wanted her to weld a curved piece on the hull. Because it was a difficult spot the fitters had not correctly positioned the huge plates and left a space about two inches wide the full width of the plate. In order to weld the space she would have to make many welds, one on top of another.

Because of her wise teacher she had been trained to understand the consequences of such a job. She knew the weld would be weak and probably break. She refused to weld it. Her commitment to doing excellent work was not well received by her co-workers. Her sub-foreman fired her on the spot for refusing to do the work.

---

[57] Shipfitters fabricate, assemble and erect all structural parts of a ship. They use heavy machinery (shears, punches, drill presses, saws, wedges and much more) to "fit" the steel plates of a ship in place. Shipfitters are also responsible for testing of tanks and compartments.

Marge knew that if she left they would just get another welder who would do the job and make a weak spot on the hull of the ship. So she sat down so no one else could work there. You might say she did the original "sit in". More than one person told her that she was fired. Finally someone came along who had the sense to check what she would not weld and told the fitters, *"You guys fix that!"* The shipfitters did what they should have done in the first place and *then* she welded it.

Later she was sometimes responsible for assisting inspectors as they went over finished work. She would burn out and replace bad welds with good. Her commitment to excellence paid off.

Marge knew that I might be one of the people coming home on that very ship and she was not willing to risk my life or the life of anyone in the Navy on such sloppy work. So you Navy guys *better* be glad. I know I am!

I cannot tell the entire shipyard story because I was not there. But I do know that there was a period of time when my little Marge worked seven days per week and ten hour days carrying heavy loads in heat and cold. As if it wasn't already hot enough doing the welding, she says, "It got to 105° one day."

She tells me of finding a board to stand on because the deck was so hot it burned her feet through her boots. At the other extreme, she worked in the east wind with ice in the rain. She tells me of getting an extension cord and hanging a light bulb down inside her jacket to keep warm.

One rainy day when her job was an overhead weld on the outside of the ship she worked with water running down her arms and into her jacket. It was her job and she just had to stay and do it. *Hats off to her!*

There were no medals given, no benefits received, few accolades awarded, but people like my wife Marge, my father Harold, and my sister Lorraine did our country a great service, sometimes at great cost to themselves.

Appendix ~ Photos

William C. Kitchen

THIS PICTURE WAS TAKEN AT THE NATIONAL GUARD AUDITORIUM ON 139th AVE NEAR MARINE DRIVE AT THE "MASSING OF THE COLORS" IN PROBABLY 2005 IT WAS BROUGHT OUT FROM THE FILES & USED AGAIN ABOUT NOV. 11, 2006. W.C.K.

Veterans in uniform will participate in a ceremony Sunday at Lone Fir Cemetery in Southeast.

OREGONIAN FILE PHOTO/2003

2005 11th Airborne reunion at Reno

Made in the USA
Charleston, SC
23 November 2014